Mike McGrath

PHP 7

in
easy steps

In easy steps is an imprint of In Easy Steps Limited
16 Hamilton Terrace · Holly Walk · Leamington Spa
Warwickshire · United Kingdom · CV32 4LY
www.ineasysteps.com

Notice of Liability
Every effort has been made to ensure that this book contains accurate
and current information. However, In Easy Steps Limited and the
author shall not be liable for any loss or damage suffered by readers
as a result of any information contained herein.

Trademarks
All trademarks are acknowledged as belonging to their respective
companies.

In Easy Steps Limited supports The Forest Stewardship Council (FSC),
the leading international forest certification organization. All our titles
that are printed on Greenpeace approved FSC certified paper carry the
FSC logo.

MIX
Paper from
responsible sources
FSC® C020837

Printed and bound in the United Kingdom

ISBN 978-1-84078-718-4

Contents

1 Getting started

Introducing PHP

The most appealing modern websites provide a customized user experience by dynamically responding to some current condition – user name, time of day, latest blog, shopping cart contents, etc. Many of these dynamic websites are created using PHP.

What is PHP?

PHP is a widely-used general purpose scripting language that is especially suited for web development and can be embedded into HTML. It was created by programmer Rasmus Lerdorf, as a set of scripts to maintain his website that he released as "Personal Home Page Tools (PHP Tools) version 1.0" on June 8, 1995.

The tools were extended in the version 2 release of 1997, and the name changed to become a recursive acronym "PHP: Hypertext Preprocessor" in version 3 the following year. Performance, reliability and extensibility was improved in 2000 with the release of PHP4, which was powered by the Zend engine virtual machine.

Subsequently, PHP5 was released in 2004 powered by the new Zend II engine and produced as free software by the PHP group. A planned experimental version PHP6, that intended to introduce native Unicode support throughout PHP was abandoned. The current version PHP7 was released in 2015, and is powered by the latest Zend 3 engine that offers improved performance. Today PHP is installed on over 20 million websites and 1 million web servers.

Why is PHP popular?

- PHP is extremely simple for a newcomer, but offers many advanced features for a professional programmer.

- PHP code is enclosed in special start and end processing tags that allow you to jump into and out of "PHP mode", to implement instructions within an HTML document.

- PHP code is executed on the server ("server-side"), unlike JavaScript code that is executed in the browser ("client-side"). The client receives the results of running the script without knowing what the underlying code was. Recently, server-side has become to be known as "The Cloud".

This is the official logo of the PHP project – the official online home of PHP can be found at php.net

This is the "elePHPant" – the mascot of the PHP project, designed by Vincent Pontier.

The New icon pictured above appears in this book to indicate new features introduced in PHP version 7.

Understanding The Cloud

Whenever a user asks to view a web page in their browser, it requests the page from the web server and receives the page in response, via the HTTP protocol. Where a web page contains PHP script, the web server will first call upon the PHP engine to process the code before sending the response to the web browser:

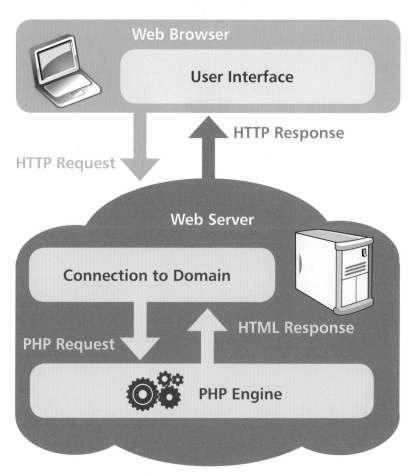

HTTP (HyperText Transfer Protocol) is the common communication standard that allows any computer connected to any web server to access files across the web.

The ensuing pages describe how to create a development environment for interactive websites by installing the following server-side technologies on your own computer:

- **Web Server** – Abyss Web Server X1 Free Personal Edition

- **PHP Engine** – PHP 7.0.4

The examples in this book are created and tested with these software versions but may require modification for other versions.

Further guidance on installation of the Abyss Web Server is available at aprelium.com/ abyssws/start.html

The Abyss setup package for Windows is an executable file named **abwsx1.exe** that you run to install the web server.

Installing the Abyss server

Abyss X1 is a free compact web server available for Windows, Mac OS X, and Linux operating systems available for download at **aprelium.com**
Despite its small footprint, Abyss supports many powerful features including dynamic content generation with server-side scripts – so is an ideal companion for PHP.

The Abyss Web Server can be installed on your own computer to provide an environment for interactive PHP website development:

1 Download the Abyss X1 Web Server setup package for your system from **aprelium.com/abyssws/download.php**

Download the Personal Edition (Free - No expiration)

The latest version is **Abyss Web Server X1 (version 2.9.3.6)**

Download Abyss Web Server X1 for Windows (2136 KB)
(The setup package contains both 32-bit and 64-bit editions.)

Download Abyss Web Server X1 for Mac OS X (3082 KB)
(Universal Binary)

Download Abyss Web Server X1 for Linux (2098 KB)
(The setup package contains both 32-bit and 64-bit editions.)

2 Run the setup installer and **Agree** the License terms, then select the Abyss Web Server component and click **Next**

Abyss Web Server X1 Setup: Installation Options — □ ×

This will install Abyss Web Server X1 on your computer.

Select components to install:
- ☑ Abyss Web Server (64-bit)
- ☐ SSL Support
- ☐ ASP.NET Support
- ☐ Documentation
- ☐ Start Menu Shortcuts

Space required: 1.2MB

Cancel   Version 2.9.3.6   < Back   Next >

3 Accept the suggested location of **C:\Abyss Web Server** then choose to **Install as a Windows Service**

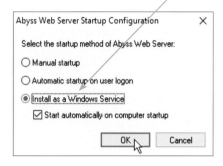

After the installation process completes, your system's default web browser will open, displaying the Abyss Web Server Console.

If you choose the "Manual startup" option, the Abyss logo will not appear in your system tray for easy start/stop control and access to the server console. Instead, the console can be found with your browser at http://localhost:9999 or numerically at http://127.0.0.1:9999 ("localhost" is an alias for the IP address 127.0.0.1).

4 Select your preferred language, then enter a name and password for future access to the Abyss Console

5 Now, log in using your chosen name and password to see the Abyss Console confirm the server Status as "Running"

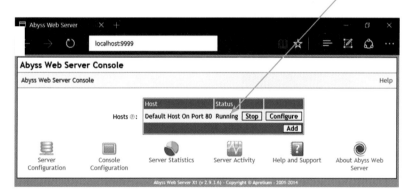

In the Abyss console, click the "Configure" button then the General icon to see the default HTTP Port is 80 and the default Documents Path (where your web pages will reside) is **/htdocs**

6 Type **http://localhost** into your browser address field then hit **Enter** – to see the default Abyss "Welcome" page

Installing the PHP engine

The PHP interpreter "engine", which implements PHP scripts within web pages, is available for Windows, Mac OS X and Linux operating systems as a free download at **php.net**

Additionally, a pre-configured package for the Abyss Web Server on Windows is available from **aprelium.com** and is recommended for a simple fast installation:

Further guidance on installation of PHP is available at **php.net/manual/en/install.php**

1 Download the PHP setup package for your system from **aprelium.com/downloads**

2 Run the downloaded executable file to launch the Setup Wizard then click on the **Next** button to begin

If you are installing PHP for Abyss on Windows from **php.net**, be sure to choose one of the VC14 Thread Safe versions – as they require fewer Windows dependencies.

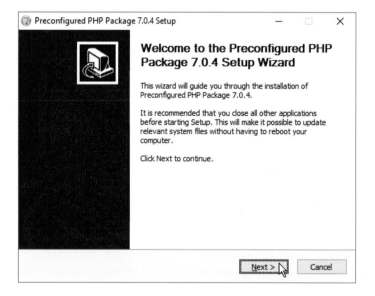

3 Next, accept the License terms then click on the **Next** button to proceed with the installation

> If you accept the terms of the agreement, click the check box below. You must accept the agreement to install Preconfigured PHP Package 7.0.4. Click Next to continue.
>
> ☑ I accept the terms of the License Agreement
>
> Packaged by Aprelium
>
> < Back   Next >   Cancel

4 Accept the suggested Destination Folder located at
C:\Program Files (X86)\PHP7 then click the **Install** button

Preconfigured PHP Package 7.0.4 Setup — □ ✕

Choose Install Location
Choose the folder in which to install Preconfigured PHP Package 7.0.4.

Setup will install Preconfigured PHP Package 7.0.4 in the following folder. To install in a
different folder, click Browse and select another folder. Click Install to start the installation.

Destination Folder

C:\Program Files (x86)\PHP7   Browse...

Space required: 55.2MB
Space available: 123.2GB

Packaged by Aprelium

< Back   Install   Cancel

Hot tip

The PHP installation location will be required when configuring the Abyss Web Server to integrate with PHP – make a note of the Destination Folder.

5 Finally, after the installation completes, click on the
Finish button to close the Setup Wizard

Preconfigured PHP Package 7.0.4 Setup — □ ✕

Completing the Preconfigured PHP Package 7.0.4 Setup Wizard

Preconfigured PHP Package 7.0.4 has been installed on your computer.

Click Finish to close this wizard.

< Back   Finish   Cancel

Don't forget

Following installation of PHP, the web server cannot yet execute PHP scripts until it is configured to recognize them and to find the PHP interpreter engine – all as described on the next page.

Integrating Abyss and PHP

The Abyss Web Server must be configured to recognize PHP scripts and employ the PHP interpreter when it encounters them. This is achieved in the Abyss Console by associating the file extension ".php" as being PHP scripts, and by specifying the location of the PHP engine on your system to interpret them:

1 Enter **http://localhost:9999** into your browser address field to launch the Abyss Web Server Console, then click the **Configure** button – to open the Configuration page

Further guidance on configuration of the Abyss Web Server is available online at aprelium.com/abyssws/start.html

2 Click on the **Scripting Parameters** icon – to open the Scripting Parameters page for editing

3 Ensure that the **Enable Scripts Execution** box is checked, then click the **Add** button in the Interpreters table – to open the Interpreters-Add page

4 Set the **Interface** parameter to "FastCGI (Local - Pipes)"

To clarify the code examples in this book components of the PHP language are colored **blue**, programmer-specified names are **red**, numeric and string data is **black**, and comments are **green**.

5 Set the **Interpreter** parameter to the PHP path location on your system of the **php-cgi.exe** file

6 Set the **Associated Extensions** parameter to "php", so your configuration should look like that shown below:

The **localhost** domain name is an alias for the domain IP address of **127.0.0.1** – so the Abyss Web Server Console can alternatively be addressed as **http://127.0.0.1:9999**

14

7 Click the **OK** button to validate your new configuration

8 Click the **Restart** button that next appears to apply the changes you have made to the Abyss configuration

Documents can only be interpreted by the PHP engine if served up by the web server using the HTTP protocol. You cannot simply open a PHP file in your browser directly. Always use the location **http://localhost/** to serve the examples in this book.

The Abyss Web Server should now be running on your system, correctly configured to recognize that documents having the **.php** file extension should be interpreted by the PHP engine. Configuration can now be tested by creating a simple PHP script for service to your web browser by Abyss:

1 Open a plain text editor and exactly type the script below
`<?php  phpinfo() ;  ?>`

phpinfo.php

2 Save the script as **phpinfo.php** in the Abyss document path directory, typically at **C:\Abyss Web Server\htdocs**

3 Exactly enter the location **http://localhost/phpinfo.php** into your web browser's address field to see Abyss serve up a web page containing your PHP version information

Hot tip

The source code of all examples in this book is available for free download at **http://www.ineasysteps.com/resource-center/downloads**.

PHP Version 7.0.4	
System	Windows NT MIKES-LAPTOP 10.0 build 10586 (Windows 10) i586
Build Date	Mar 2 2016 14:40:59
Compiler	MSVC14 (Visual C++ 2015)
Architecture	x86
Configure Command	cscript /nologo configure.js "--enable-snapshot-build" "--enable-debug-pack" "--with-pdo-oci=c:\php-sdk\oracle\x86\instantclient_12_1\sdk,shared" "--with-oci8-12c=c:\php-sdk\oracle\x86\instantclient_12_1\sdk,shared" "--enable-object-out-dir=../obj/" "--enable-com-dotnet=shared" "--with-mcrypt=static" "--without-analyzer" "--with-pgo"
Server API	CGI/FastCGI
Virtual Directory Support	enabled
Configuration File (php.ini) Path	C:\WINDOWS
Loaded Configuration File	C:\Program Files (x86)\PHP7\php.ini
Scan this dir for additional .ini files	(none)
Additional .ini files parsed	(none)
PHP API	20151012

Beware

PHP scripts are case-sensitive so you must copy the listed script using lowercase characters only.

Embedding PHP script code

PHP script may be embedded within HTML documents – meaning PHP and HTML code can both happily co-exist in the same file. All embedded PHP code must be contained within **<?php** and **?>** tags so it can be readily recognized by the PHP engine for interpretation. Typically the PHP code will write content into the body section of the HTML document, which is then sent to the web browser:

hello.php

1 Launch a plain text editor and create this valid barebones HTML5 document with an empty body section
```
<!DOCTYPE HTML>
<html lang="en">
<head>
<meta charset="UTF-8">
<title>Getting Started In PHP</title>
</head>
<body>

</body>
</html>
```

2 Insert tags into the body section to contain PHP code
```
<?php

?>
```

3 Now, insert between the PHP tags a descriptive comment and a line of code to write content into the body section
```
# Write the traditional greeting.
echo '<h1>Hello World!</h1>' ;
```

Hot tip

Notice that the descriptive comment is enclosed between the PHP tags for information purposes only.

```
≡    Code Writer                              ⤢   —   □   ×
 1  <!DOCTYPE HTML>
 2  <html lang="en">
 3  <head>
 4  <meta charset="UTF-8">
 5  <title>Getting Started In PHP</title>
 6  </head>
 7  <body>
 8  <?php
 9  #Write the traditional greeting.
10  echo '<h1>Hello World!</h1>' ;
11  ?>
12  </body>
13  </html>
```

...cont'd

4 Set the document encoding to UTF-8 format then save it as **hello.php** in the Abyss server's **/htdocs** folder

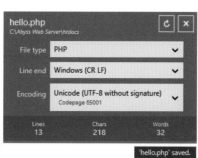

Beware

Windows' Notepad automatically adds a hidden "Byte Order Mark" (BOM) signature to the file, while other editors (such as Code Writer shown here) allow this to be omitted. Code Writer is a free text and code editor available from the Windows Store.

5 Next, enter the location **http://localhost/hello.php** into your web browser's address field to see Abyss serve up a web page containing content written by embedded PHP code

6 Now, use your web browser's **View Source** facility to see that PHP has written the content into the body section, including the HTML **<h1></h1>** heading tags

Don't forget

Note that the PHP **echo** instruction literally writes the entire content contained within the pair of **' '** single quote marks.

PHP script can be embedded in earlier versions of HTML in just the same way. Other examples in this book demonstrate embedded PHP script but do not repeatedly list the HTML code.

Scripting by the rules

Tag rules

When the PHP engine receives input from the web server it reads the input, from top to bottom, in a process called "parsing". During the parsing process, the PHP engine (a.k.a. parser) looks for the opening and closing **<?php** and **?>** tags and understands that the content between those tags is script code that it must interpret. Everything outside the **<?php** and **?>** tags is completely ignored, which allows PHP files to have mixed content and allows PHP code to be embedded within HTML like this:

```
<p>Ignored by PHP and displayed by the browser</p>
```

```
<?php echo 'Script code that will be parsed' ; ?>
```

```
<p>Also ignored by PHP and displayed by the browser</p>
```

In order for this to work properly it is therefore important that all your PHP script code must be enclosed between opening and closing **<?php** and **?>** tags, when embedded in an HTML file.

The only exception to this rule is when PHP script is written in a pure PHP file, which contains only code. In this case it is preferable to omit the closing **?>** tag like this:

```
<?php  echo 'Print this First' ;
       echo 'Print this Last' ;
```

Where your PHP script code intends only to insert a single string of text into an HTML document, you may optionally use the PHP short echo **<?=** and **?>** tags:

<?= 'Hello!' ; ?> is equivalent to **<?php echo 'Hello!' ; ?>**

Advanced PHP script code can also insert text only when a tested condition is met, like this:

```
<?php if ( $expression == true ) : ?>

        Insert this text only if the expression is true.

<?php else : ?>

        Otherwise insert this text.

<?php endif ; ?>
```

Statement rules

Each statement within the PHP language must be terminated by a **;** semicolon character – just as each sentence in the English language must be terminated by a **.** period character. The semicolon is recognized by the parser as marking the end of an individual instruction that it must interpret. So a PHP code block containing two statements could look like this:

```php
<?php echo 'First statement' ; echo 'Second statement' ; ?>
```

The closing **?>** tag of a block of PHP code automatically implies a semicolon, however, so you can optionally omit the semicolon terminating the last statement of a PHP block, like this:

```php
<?php echo 'First statement' ; echo 'Second statement' ?>
```

It does no harm to terminate the last statement of a PHP block if you wish to do so.

Comment rules

It is often worthwhile adding comments to your PHP script code so it can be more easily understood by others, or by yourself when revisiting your code later. All whitespace and comments are completely ignored by the PHP parser so you can add as many comments as you like, without any adverse effect on performance.

Single-line comments may begin with a **#** hash character, or alternatively they may begin with a **//** double-slash sequence.

Multi-line (block) comments must be enclosed within **/*** and ***/** character sequences, as used in the C programming language:

```php
<?php
        echo 'First statement' ; // A single-line comment.

        /* This is a multi-line comment
        containing two lines of comment. */

        echo 'Second statement' ;

    echo 'Final statement' ; # Another single-line comment.

?>
```

The **//** single-line comment style is also used in C++ programming and the **#** single-line comment style is also used in Unix/Linux BASH shell scripting.

Summary

- PHP is a scripting language that is especially suited for web development as it can be embedded in HTML

- PHP code is executed server-side on The Cloud, unlike JavaScript code that is executed client-side in the browser

- Where a web page contains PHP script, the web server will first call upon the PHP engine to process the code before sending the response to the web browser

- A local development environment can be created by installing a web server and the PHP engine on your own computer

- The **http://localhost** URL is an alias for the numerical IP address of **http://127.0.0.1**

- Access to the Abyss Web Server Console requires your user name and password, and is found at **http://localhost:9999**

- A pre-configured package for the Abyss Web Server is recommended for simple fast installation of the PHP engine

- The Web Server must be configured to recognize scripts so it will direct them to the PHP engine, by setting Interface, Interpreter, and Associated Extension parameters

- The PHP code instruction **phpinfo()** can be used to serve up a web page containing your PHP version information

- Documents containing PHP script can best be encoded using the popular UTF-8 character format

- The PHP **echo** instruction literally writes the text content contained within following quote marks

- All embedded PHP code must be enclosed within **<?php** and **?>** tags so it can be recognized by the PHP engine

- Each statement within the PHP language must be terminated by a **;** semicolon character

- Single-line comments may begin with a **#** hash character or with a **//** double-slash sequence

- Multi-line block comments must be enclosed within **/*** and ***/** character sequences

2 Storing values

This chapter demonstrates the various PHP containers in which data can be stored.

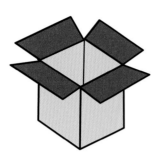

Beware

In PHP **$this** is a special variable so you cannot use 'this' as a variable name.

Don't forget

Variables that are accessible throughout the script must have unique names. See page 74 for more on 'variable scope'.

Beware

Do not confuse the purpose of double and single quotes. Remember that PHP only makes variable substitutions for mixed strings enclosed within double quotes.

Creating variables

A "variable" is a named container in a PHP script in which a data value can be stored. The stored value can be referenced using the variable's name and changed (varied) as the script proceeds. The script author can choose any name for a variable providing it adheres to these three naming conventions:

- Names must begin with a $ dollar sign – for example **$name**

- Names can comprise letters, numbers and underscore characters, but not spaces – for example **$subtotal_1**

- The first character after the $ dollar sign must be a letter or an underscore character – it cannot be a number

Note that variable names in PHP are case-sensitive, so **$name**, **$Name** and **$NAME** are three separate individual variables.

PHP variables are "loosely typed" meaning they can contain data of any type, unlike "strongly typed" variables in some languages, where the data type must be specified when the variable is created. So a PHP variable may happily contain an integer number, or a floating-point number, or a string of text characters, or a Boolean value of **TRUE** or **FALSE**, or an object, or a **NULL** empty value.

A variable is created in a PHP script simply by stating its name. The variable can then be assigned an initial value (initialized) by using the = assignment operator to state its value. This statement, and all others in PHP, must end with a semi-colon like this:

$body_temp = 98.6 ;

The value contained within the variable can then be displayed by referencing it using the variable name, like this:

echo $body_temp ;

Usefully, the variable's value can be displayed as part of a mixed string by enclosing the string and variable name in <u>double quotes</u>:

echo "Body temperature is $body_temp degrees Fahrenheit" ;

The double quotes ensure that PHP will evaluate the whole string and substitute named variables with their stored values. This feature does not work if the string is enclosed in single quotes!

1 Create a valid HTML document, like the one listed on page 16, then insert PHP tags into the body section

```
<?php
  # Statements to be inserted here.
?>
```

variable.php

2 Now, insert between the PHP tags a statement to create and initialize a variable

```
$body_temp = 98.6 ;
```

3 Next, insert a statement to display the variable value alone

```
echo $body_temp ;
```

4 Then, insert a statement to display the variable value substituted in a mixed string – assigned in double quotes

```
echo "<p>Body temperature is $body_temp
                        degrees Fahrenheit " ;
```

Hot tip

Notice that variables created in the main body of a script, like the one in this example, are accessible "globally" – throughout the entire PHP script.

5 Insert a statement to assign a new value to the variable

```
$body_temp = 37.0 ;
```

6 Finally, insert a statement to display the new variable value substituted in a mixed string

```
echo "( $body_temp degrees Celsius )</p>" ;
```

Don't forget

Each statement in the PHP language must be terminated by a semi-colon – just as each statement in the English language must be terminated by a period.

7 Save the document in your web server's **/htdocs** directory as **variable.php** then open the page via HTTP to see the variable values get displayed

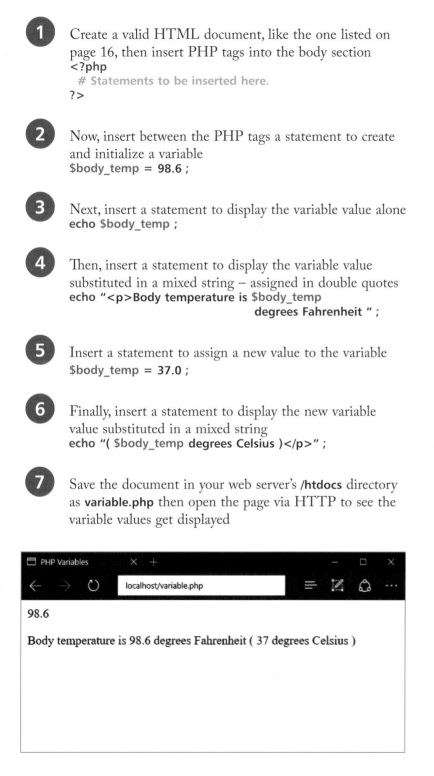

PHP Variables

localhost/variable.php

98.6

Body temperature is 98.6 degrees Fahrenheit (37 degrees Celsius)

Quoting strings

A "string" of text can be stored in a variable in much the same way as a numeric value, but the assignment must surround the string with quote marks to denote its beginning and end. Both single and double quote marks can be used for this purpose, but you must use the same type of quote marks to denote the beginning and end of the text string. For example, both these statements make valid string assignments:

$song_title = "Summertime Blues" ;

$song_title = 'Summertime Blues' ;

Where you wish to store a string of text that itself includes quote marks, you can "escape" the included quote marks by preceding them with a \ backslash character, or use the alternative type of quote mark within the string. For example, both these statements assign strings that include quote marks:

$song_title = "the \"Summertime\" aria by George Gershwin" ;

$song_title = 'the "Summertime" aria by George Gershwin' ;

The second technique, using double quote marks within the string, is easier to read and is preferred throughout this book.

String values can be displayed as part of a mixed string by enclosing the mixed string in <u>double quotes,</u> like this:

echo "Many regard $song_title as a popular classic" ;

The double quotes ensure that PHP will evaluate the mixed string and substitute named variables with their stored values. This feature does not work if the string is enclosed in single quotes!

String values can be joined together ("concatenated") into a single string using the . concatenation operator, like this:

$hi = 'Hello' ;
$bye = 'Goodbye' ;
$song_title = $hi . $bye ;   # 'HelloGoodbye'

Additionally, spaces and punctuation can usefully be inserted when concatenating strings, so the title assignment above could be modified to include a comma and a space:

$song_title = $hi . ', ' . $bye ;   # 'Hello, Goodbye'

Don't forget

Variable names cannot contain spaces – but the underscore character is often used in their place.

24

1 Create a valid HTML document, like the one listed on page 16, then insert PHP tags into the body section

```
<?php
    # Statements to be inserted here.
?>
```

string.php

2 Now, insert between the PHP tags a statement to create and initialize two variables

```
$phrase = 'The truth is rarely pure' ;
$author = 'Oscar Wilde' ;
```

3 Next, insert a statement to display a variable value alone

```
echo $phrase ;
```

4 Then, insert a statement to display the variable value substituted in a mixed string – assigned in double quotes

```
echo "<p>It is often said that <q>$phrase</q> </p>" ;
```

5 Insert a statement to concatenate a string to a variable

```
$phrase = $phrase . ' and never simple' ;
```

6 Finally, insert a statement to display both current variable values substituted in a mixed string

```
echo "<p><q>$phrase</q><cite>$author</cite></p>" ;
```

7 Save the document in your web server's **/htdocs** directory as **string.php** then open the page via HTTP to see the variable values get displayed

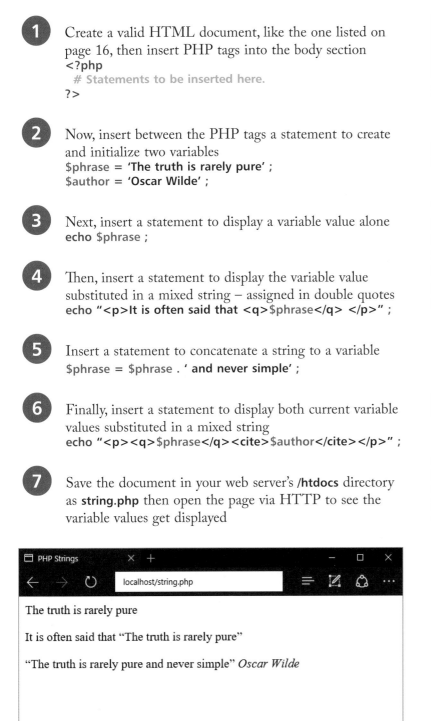

Hot tip

You can also use a shorthand concatenate assignment operator **.=** to join two strings – so that **$a = $a . $b** can be simply written as **$a .= $b**.

Hot tip

Adopt a consistent naming style for your variables – such as all lowercase **$my_var**, or "camelcase" **$myVar**.

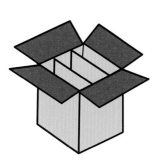

Square brackets denote "element" so are not needed after the variable name in the assignment using the **array()** function – they are only needed when addressing an element.

The **foreach** construct exists specifically for arrays and provides an easy way to traverse all array element keys and values. See pages 60-65 for more on loops.

Producing arrays

Indexed arrays

An array variable can store multiple items of data in sequential array "elements" that are numbered ("indexed") starting at zero. So the first array value is stored in array element number zero. Individual array element values can be referenced using the variable name followed by the index number in square brackets. For example, **$days[0]** references the value stored in the first array element of an array variable named "days". Similarly, **$days[1]** references the value stored in the second array element, and so on. Variable arrays can be created by making multiple statements that assign values to successive elements, or by making a single statement using a PHP **array()** function to fill the elements:

$days[] = 'Monday' ; $days[] = 'Tuesday' ; $days[] = 'Wednesday' ;
or...
$days = array('Monday' , 'Tuesday' , 'Wednesday') ;
Both create an array where the value stored in each element can be referenced using its index number, such as **$days[0]**.

Associative arrays

When creating an array, you can optionally specify a key name for each element that can be used to reference that element's value:

$months['jan'] = 'January' ;
$months['feb'] = 'February' ;
$months['mar'] = 'March' ;
or...
$months =
array('jan' => 'January' , 'feb' => 'February' , 'mar' => 'March') ;
Both create an array where the value stored in each element can be referenced using its key name, such as **$months['jan']**.

Traversing arrays

All elements of an array can be traversed using a **foreach** loop to reference each element's value in turn and assign it to a variable:

```
foreach( $months as $value )
{
  # Use the current $value on each iteration.
}
```

The keys can also be accessed on each iteration of the loop using
```
foreach( $months as $key => $value )
{
  # Use the current $key and $value on each iteration.
}
```

1 Create a valid HTML document, like the one listed on page 16, then insert PHP tags into the body section

```php
<?php
   # Statements to be inserted here.
?>
```

array.php

2 Now, insert between the PHP tags a statement to create and initialize a variable array with values

```php
$days = array( 'Monday' , 'Tuesday' , 'Wednesday' ) ;
```

Hot tip

You can set the first element key to 1, so the index will begin at one rather than zero, using
`$months = array( 1 => 'January' , 'February' , March' ) ;`

3 Next, insert a statement to display the value in all array elements as a bulleted list

```php
foreach( $days as $value ) { echo "&bull; $value " ; }
```

4 Then, insert a statement to create and initialize a variable array with both keys and values

```php
$months = array( 'jan' => 'January' ,
                 'feb' => 'February' , 'mar' => 'March' ) ;
```

5 Finally, insert statements to display the key and value in all elements as a definition list

```php
echo '<dl>' ;
foreach( $months as $key => $value )
{ echo "<dt>$key<dd>$value" ; }
echo '</dl>' ;
```

Beware

If you specify key names you cannot reference elements by their index number, and if you specify the same key name twice, the second value will overwrite the first value.

6 Save the document in your web server's **/htdocs** directory as **array.php** then open the page via HTTP to see the variable array element values get displayed

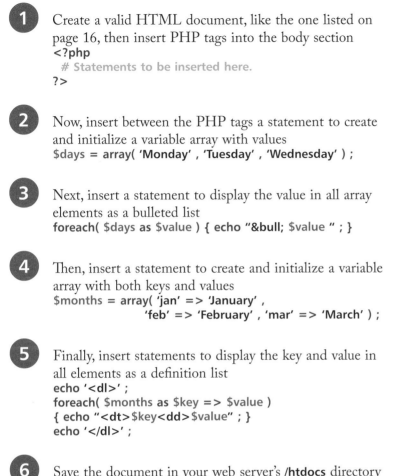

PHP Arrays

localhost/array.php

• Monday • Tuesday • Wednesday

jan
  January
feb
  February
mar
  March

Hot tip

You can easily create arrays containing sequential numbers or letters with the PHP **range()** function. For example with
`$six = range( 1 , 6 ) ;`
`$a_z = range( 'a','z' ) ;`

Sorting arrays

PHP provides two handy functions to convert between variable arrays and strings because they are so frequently used together. The **implode()** function converts an array to a string and inserts a specified separator between each value. Typically, this might be used to create a list of comma-separated values (csv) like this:

```
$csv_list = implode( ' , ' , $array ) ;
```

Conversely, the **explode()** function converts a string to an array by specifying a separator around which to break up the string. This might be used to create an array from a comma-separated list:

```
$array = explode( ' , ' . $csv_list ) ;
```

PHP also provides three useful functions to sort array elements into ascending alphanumeric order (a-z 1-9):

- **sort()** function – sorts by value discarding the original key

- **asort()** function – sorts by value retaining the original key

- **ksort()** function – sorts by key

Existing array values are sorted with a simple statement like this:

```
$makers = array( 'Ford' , 'Chevrolet' , 'Dodge' ) ;
sort( $makers ) ;
```

Array elements can also be sorted into descending alphanumeric order (9-1 z-a) with three similar functions:

- **rsort()** function – sorts by value discarding the original key

- **arsort()** function – sorts by value retaining the original key

- **krsort()** function – sorts by key

It is important to recognize that specified key names will be discarded by the **sort()** and **rsort()** functions, so these should only be used where the key/value relationship is not significant – otherwise use the **asort()** and **arsort()** functions to retain the keys.

Hot tip

You can test if a variable is an array using the **is_array()** function. For example, **is_array($var) ;**

1 Create a valid HTML document, like the one listed on page 16, then insert PHP tags into the body section
```php
<?php
  # Statements to be inserted here.
?>
```

sort.php

2 Now, insert between the PHP tags a statement to create and initialize a variable array with key names and values
```php
$cars = array( 'Dodge' => 'Viper' ,
        'Chevrolet' => 'Camaro' , 'Ford' => 'Mustang' ) ;
```

3 Next, insert statements to display all keys and values of the array as a bulleted list within a definition list
```php
echo '<dl><dt>Original Element Order :<dd>' ;
foreach( $cars as $key => $value )
{ echo ' &bull; ' , $key . ' ' . $value ; }
```

Hot tip

You can discover the number of elements in an array with a **count()** function. For example,
$num = count($array) ;

4 Then, insert statements to display the array sorted by value
```php
asort( $cars ) ;
echo '<dt>Sorted Into Value Order :<dd>' ;
foreach( $cars as $key => $value )
{ echo ' &bull; ' , $key . ' ' . $value ; }
```

5 Finally, insert statements to display the array sorted by key
```php
ksort( $cars ) ;
echo '<dt>Sorted Into Key Order :<dd>' ;
foreach( $cars as $key => $value )
{ echo ' &bull; ' , $key . ' ' . $value ; }
echo '</dl>' ;
```

Don't forget

Do not use the **sort()** or **rsort()** functions where the keys are important.

6 Save the document in your web server's **/htdocs** directory as **sort.php** then open the page via HTTP to see the sorted array values get displayed

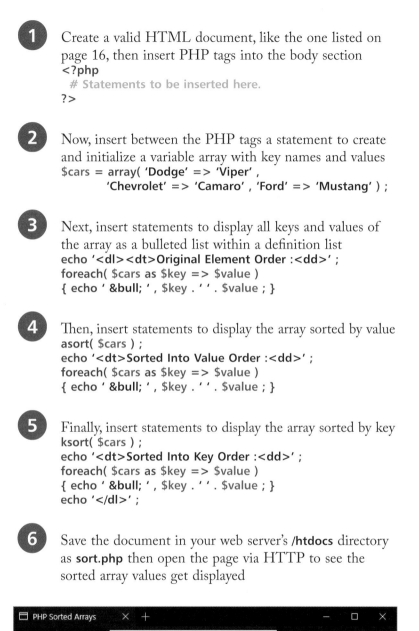

```
PHP Sorted Arrays    ×   +                    —  □  ×
←  →  ↻    localhost/sort.php          ≡  ✍  ⌾  ...

Original Element Order :
       • Dodge Viper • Chevrolet Camaro • Ford Mustang
Sorted Into Value Order :
       • Chevrolet Camaro • Ford Mustang • Dodge Viper
Sorted Into Key Order :
       • Chevrolet Camaro • Dodge Viper • Ford Mustang
```

29

Describing dimensions

The numbering of array elements is more correctly known as the "array index" and, because element numbering starts at zero, is sometimes referred to as a "zero-based index". An array created with a single index is a one-dimensional array in which the elements appear in a single row:

Element content	A	B	C	D	E
Index numbers	[0]	[1]	[2]	[3]	[4]

Arrays can also have multiple indices – to represent multiple dimensions. An array created with two indices is a two-dimensional array in which the elements appear in multiple rows:

First index	[0]	A	B	C	D	E
	[1]	F	G	H	I	J
Second index		[0]	[1]	[2]	[3]	[4]

With multi-dimensional arrays, the value contained in each element is referenced by stating the number of each index. For example, with the two-dimensional array above the element at [1][2] contains the letter H.

Two-dimensional arrays are useful to store grid-based information, such as XY coordinates. Creating a three-dimensional array, with three indices, would allow XYZ coordinates to be stored.

Creating a multi-dimensional array in PHP is simply a matter of creating an outer array, whose elements are themselves arrays. As usual you may optionally specify a key name for each element – in this case to represent each inner array. Individual values can then be referenced using the key name and inner index number:

$matrix['Letter'][0]

It is, however, necessary to always enclose array variables that use quoted keys within curly braces when included in a string:

echo "Element value is {$matrix['Letter'][0]} " ;

All inner arrays in a multi-dimensional array can be accessed using a **foreach** loop to iterate through the arrays. A nested **foreach** loop can then reference each element in turn.

Beware

Multi-dimensional arrays with more than two indices can produce hard to read source code and may lead to errors.

1 Create a valid HTML document, like the one listed on page 16, then insert PHP tags into the body section

```php
<?php
  # Statements to be inserted here.
?>
```

matrix.php

2 Now, insert between the PHP tags a statement to create and initialize two regular variable arrays and a two-dimensional array with key names

```php
$letters = array( 'A' , 'B' , 'C' ) ;
$numbers = array( 1 , 2 , 3 ) ;
$matrix =
array( 'Letter' => $letters , 'Number' => $numbers ) ;
```

Hot tip

Multi-dimensional arrays are more common than you might think. For example, an HTML form that allows multiple selections for inputs with the same name are submitted as a multi-dimensional array.

3 Next, insert a statement to display a single stored value

```php
echo "<p>Start : {$matrix['Letter'][0]} </p>" ;
```

4 Finally, insert statements to display the key and value in all elements as two unordered lists

```php
foreach( $matrix as $array => $list )
{
  echo '<ul>' ;
  foreach( $list as $key => $value )
  { echo "<li>$array [ $key ] = $value " ; }
  echo '</ul>' ;
}
```

5 Save the document in your web server's **/htdocs** directory as **matrix.php** then open the page via HTTP to see the variable array values get displayed

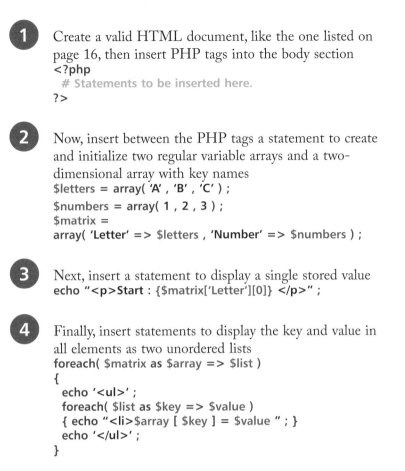

Don't forget

Array variables that use quoted keys must be enclosed within curly braces when included in a string.

Checking types

PHP variables can store various types of data so it is useful to clearly understand each data type in detail:

- **string** – a series of characters in which each character is the size of one byte, up to a maximum length of 2GB. Strings enclosed in single quotes are treated as literals, whereas strings in double quotes will interpret special characters

- **int** – a non-decimal number between 2,147,483,648 and -2,147,483,647, specified as a decimal (10-based), hexadecimal (16-based – prefixed with 0x), or octal (8-based – prefixed with 0)

- **float** – a floating-point decimal number or a number in exponential format. A float is also known as a "double"

- **bool** – an expression of a Boolean truth value, which may be only true or false

- **array** – an ordered map of multiple data values that associates keys to values. The keys are index numbered by default or may be explicitly-specified labels

- **object** – a class containing stored data properties and providing methods to process data

- **resource** – a reference to an external resource that is created and used by special functions

- **NULL** – a variable with no value whatsoever. It may have not been initialized, have been assigned the **NULL** constant, or have been nullified by the PHP **unset()** function

The data type of any item can be checked by specifying it as the argument to the **gettype()** function. For example, where a variable **$num** contains an integer value, **gettype($num)** will return "integer" and where a variable **$str** contains a string value, **gettype($str)** will return "string", and so on. Where the data type cannot be identified the **gettype()** function will return "unknown type".

Perhaps more usefully, the **var_dump()** function can check an item's data type and will dump structured information that displays its type and value.

Hot tip

The creation and use of PHP class objects are demonstrated fully in Chapter 7.

...cont'd

1 Create a valid HTML document, like the one listed on page 16, then insert PHP tags into the body section
```php
<?php
  # Statements to be inserted here.
?>
```

types.php

2 Next, insert between the PHP tags a statement to create a filestream resource and an array
```php
$filestream = fopen( 'index.html' , 'r' ) ;
$data = array( 'PHP' , 1 , 2.3 , TRUE , NULL , array() ,
                        new Directory , $filestream ) ;
```

Hot tip

The creation and use of PHP filestream resources are demonstrated fully in Chapter 8.

3 Now, insert a statement to display the data type stored within each array element
```php
foreach( $data as $type )
{
  var_dump( $type ) ;
  echo '<br> ' ;
}
```

4 Finally, insert statements to destroy the filestream resource then attempt to get its data type once more
```php
fclose( $filestream ) ;
echo gettype( $filestream ) ;
```

5 Save the document in your web server's **/htdocs** directory as **types.php** then open the page via HTTP to see the data types and values get displayed

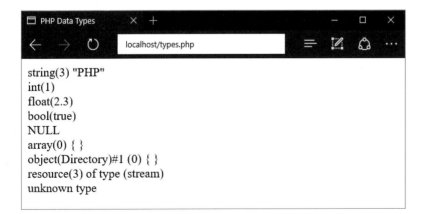

Hot tip

The Boolean constants **TRUE** and **FALSE** are not case-sensitive, so may be written as **true** and **false**.

33

Defining constants

Fixed data values that will never change in a script should be stored in a PHP "constant", rather than in a variable. A constant is a named container in which numeric or string values can be stored and can be referenced using the constant's name.

When creating a variable, always consider whether its value will ever change – if it will not you should create a constant instead. For example, **define('PI' , 3.14) ;**

Unlike a variable, a constant cannot contain Boolean values of **TRUE** or **FALSE,** nor represent an object, nor a **NULL** empty value. Additionally, a constant cannot be changed as the script proceeds. This safeguards the constant value from accidental alteration and is good programming practice.

Constant names are subject to the same naming conventions as variables, but it is traditional to use uppercase characters for constant names – to easily distinguish them from variable names. Constants are created using a **define()** function to specify the constant's name and the value it will contain, like this:

define('NAME' , value) ;

Most significantly, constant names are <u>not</u> prefixed by a $ dollar sign, so they cannot be included in mixed strings for display – as PHP cannot distinguish a constant name from a regular capitalized string. Consider these statements for example:

define('USER' , 'Mike') ;
echo "Hello USER"

...the output here is **Hello USER** , not **Hello Mike** as desired.

In order to include a constant's value in an output string it must be referenced separately and "concatenated" to the string with the PHP . concatenation operator, like this:

echo 'Hello ' . USER ;

...the output here is now **Hello Mike** as desired.

Array constants, in which all elements contain fixed data values, can also be created using the **define()** function like this:

define('WEEKDAYS' , ['Mon', 'Tue' , 'Wed' , 'Thu' , 'Fri']) ;

The ability to create constant arrays with the **define()** function is new in PHP 7.

Constants defined by the script author can be used just like the predefined constants that are built into PHP, such as **PHP_VERSION** and **PHP_OS** that describe the version and server operating system.

1 Create a valid HTML document, like the one listed on page 16, then insert PHP tags into the body section

```
<?php
  # Statements to be inserted here.
?>
```

2 Now, insert between the PHP tags a statement to create and initialize a constant

```
define( 'USER' , 'Mike' ) ;
```

3 Add a statement to create and initialize an array constant

```
define( 'PETS' , [ 'Kitten' , 'Puppy' , 'Hamster' ] ) ;
```

4 Next, insert a statement to display two constant values in a concatenated string

```
echo '<p>Hello ' . USER . ' how is your ' . PETS[1] . '?</p>' ;
```

5 Insert a statement to display the predefined constant value of the PHP version in a concatenated string

```
echo '<p>You are using PHP version ' . PHP_VERSION ;
```

6 Finally, insert a statement to display the predefined constant value of the host operating system in a string

```
echo ' running on ' . PHP_OS . '</p>' ;
```

7 Save the document in your web server's **/htdocs** directory as **constant.php** then open the page via HTTP to see the results get displayed

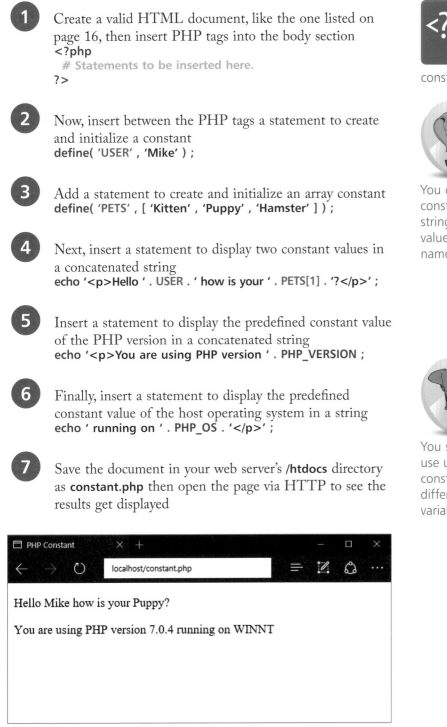

constant.php

You cannot include constants in mixed strings, or change their value, or begin their name with a dollar sign.

You should always use uppercase for constant names to easily differentiate them from variables in your code.

The **$_FILES** superglobal is used by the file upload example on page 138.

The **$_POST** superglobal is used by the HTML form submission example on page 124.

The **$_COOKIE** superglobal is used by the example on page 148 to get data from a cookie on the user's computer.

The **$_SESSION** superglobal is used by the example on page 153 to store data on the web server.

Exploring superglobals

PHP provides several pre-defined variables that are always globally available anywhere within any script. These are aptly known as "superglobals" and are described briefly here:

● **$GLOBALS** – an associative array containing references to all variables which are currently defined in the global scope of the script, according to context. The variable names are the keys of this associative array. For example:
foreach($GLOBALS as $key => $var) echo "• $key "

PHP GLOBALS   ×   +   — □ ×

← → ↻ | http://localhost/globals.php   ▢ ☆ | ☰ ◪ ◌ ⋯

• _GET • _POST • _COOKIE • _FILES • GLOBALS • var • key

● **$_SERVER** – an array containing information such as headers, paths and script locations, that is arbitrarily provided by the web server

● **$_GET** – an associative array of variables passed to the script by appended URL parameters

● **$_POST** – an associative array of variables passed to the script by the HTTP POST method

● **$_FILES** – an associative array of uploaded file items passed to the script by the HTTP POST method

● **$_COOKIE** – an associative array of variables passed to the script via HTTP from cookies on the user's computer

● **$_SESSION** – an associative array containing variables available to each script on a website until the user exits

● **$_REQUEST** – an associative array that by default contains the contents of **$_GET**, **$_POST** and **$_COOKIE**

● **$_ENV** – an associative array of variables passed to the current script by the shell environment under which the PHP parser is running. Different systems will run different kinds of shells

1 Create a valid HTML document, like the one listed on page 16, then insert PHP tags into the body section
```
<?php
   # Statements to be inserted here.
?>
```

supers.php

2 Now, insert between the PHP tags a statement to display your server software details
```
echo 'Web Server : '.$_SERVER[ 'SERVER_SOFTWARE' ].'<br>' ;
```

3 Add a statement to display this script name
```
echo 'This Script : '.$_SERVER[ 'PHP_SELF' ].'<br>' ;
```

4 Next, insert statements to display the host name and the page request method
```
echo 'Host Name : '.$_SERVER[ 'HTTP_HOST' ].'<br>' ;
echo 'Request Method : '.$_SERVER[ 'REQUEST_METHOD' ] ;
```

Hot tip

$_SERVER['PHP_SELF'] is used by the example on page 136 to create a "sticky" HTML form.

5 Insert a statement to display appended URL parameters
```
foreach( $_GET as $key => $value )
{ echo '<hr>HTTP GET : '.$key.'='.$value ; }
```

6 Save the document in your web server's **/htdocs** directory as **supers.php**

Hot tip

$_SERVER['REQUEST_METHOD'] is used by the example on page 134 to establish whether an HTML form has been submitted by a user.

7 Open the page via HTTP by appending parameters to the script name in the browser address field, such as "?name=mike&lang=PHP", to see them pass to the script

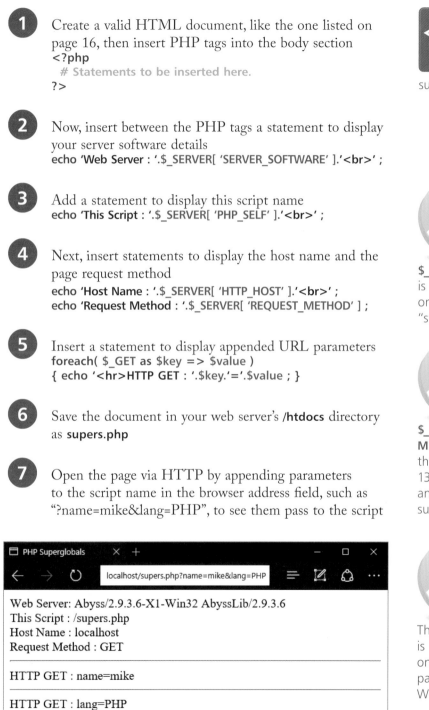

PHP Superglobals

localhost/supers.php?name=mike&lang=PHP

Web Server: Abyss/2.9.3.6-X1-Win32 AbyssLib/2.9.3.6
This Script : /supers.php
Host Name : localhost
Request Method : GET

HTTP GET : name=mike

HTTP GET : lang=PHP

37

Hot tip

The HTTP **GET** method is used by the example on page 182 to set parameters for an XML Web Service response.

Summary

- A variable is a named container in which changeable data can be stored

- The value stored in a variable can be referenced using that variable's name

- Variable names must begin with a **$** dollar sign, may comprise letters, numbers and underscore characters, and the first character after the **$** must only be a letter or an underscore

- A variable can store an integer number, floating-point number, text string, Boolean value, object, or **NULL** value

- A variable is initialized using the = assignment operator to assign an initial value to that variable

- A variable's value can be displayed as part of a mixed string by enclosing the string and variable name in double quotes only

- Strings may be enclosed in either single quotes or double quotes, and inner quote marks can be escaped using a backslash

- String values can be joined together into a single string using the . concatenation operator

- An array variable can store multiple items of data in sequential array elements that are numbered starting at zero by default

- Optionally, key names may be specified for each array element

- A **foreach** loop can be used to traverse each element in an array

- The **implode()** and **explode()** functions convert between strings and arrays by adding or removing specified separators

- Arrays can be sorted into alphanumeric order by value or key

- A multi-dimensional array is simply an array whose element values are themselves arrays

- The **gettype()** and **var_dump()** functions can be used to check data types

- A constant is a named container in which a fixed integer, floating-point number, or text string can be stored

- Constant names are not prefixed by a **$** and are all uppercase

- A constant is initialized using the **define()** function

- Superglobal variables are always globally available anywhere within any script

3 Performing operations

This chapter demonstrates the various PHP operators for arithmetic, comparison and logical evaluation.

Doing arithmetic

The arithmetic operators commonly used in PHP scripts are listed in the table below, together with the operation they perform:

Operator:	Operation:
+	Addition
-	Subtraction
*	Multiplication
/	Division
%	Modulus
**	Exponentiation

The numbers used along with operators to form expressions are known as "operands" – in the expression **2 + 3** the numbers **2** and **3** are the operands.

Don't forget

Group expressions with parentheses to specify evaluation precedence – innermost groups get evaluated first. See page 51 for more on operator precedence.

Operators for addition, subtraction, multiplication and division act as you would expect. Care must be taken, however, to group expressions for clarity where more than one operator is used:

```
a = b * c - d % e / f ;          # This is unclear.

a = ( b * c ) - ( ( d % e ) / f ) ;   # This is clearer.
```

The **%** modulus operator divides the first given number by the second given number and returns the remainder of the operation. This is useful to determine if a number has an odd or even value.

The ****** exponentiation operator gives the result of raising the first operand to the power of the second operand.

```
a ** b          # Result of raising a to the b'th power
```

Shorthand expressions can usefully be created by combining an arithmetic operator with the = assignment operator. For example:

```
a += b ;        # Equivalent to a = ( a + b ) ;
a -= b ;        # Equivalent to a = ( a - b ) ;
a *= b ;        # Equivalent to a = ( a * b ) ;
a /= b ;        # Equivalent to a = ( a / b ) ;
```

...cont'd

1 Create a valid HTML document, like the one listed on page 16, then insert PHP tags into the body section
```php
<?php
 # Statements to be inserted here.
?>
```

arithmetic.php

2 Now, insert statements between the PHP tags to create and initialize two variables
```php
$a = 5 ;
$b = 2 ;
```

3 Next, insert statements to display the results of simple arithmetical operations using the variable values
```php
$result = $a + $b ; echo "Addition : $result <br>" ;
$result = $a - $b ; echo "Subtraction : $result <br>" ;
$result = $a * $b ; echo "Multiplication : $result <br>" ;
$result = $a / $b ; echo "Division : $result <br>" ;
```

4 Finally, insert a statement to display the results of arithmetical evaluations of the variable values
```php
$result = $a % $b ; echo "Modulus : $result <br>" ;
$result = $a ** $b ; echo "Exponentiation : $result" ;
```

5 Save the document in your web server's **/htdocs** directory as **arithmetic.php** then open the page via HTTP to see the results and variable values get displayed

```
PHP Arithmetic       ×   +              —   □   ×
←   →   ○     localhost/arithmetic.php        ≡  ✒  ♢  ...

Addition : 7
Subtraction : 3
Multiplication : 10
Division : 2.5
Modulus : 1
Exponentiation : 25
```

Hot tip

PHP has some useful functions to work with numbers. For example, **round($a)** rounds **$a** to the nearest integer and **number_format($a)** adds commas to **$a** denoting groups of thousands.

NEW

PHP 7 introduces a new **intdiv()** function that performs an integer division on two operands and returns an integer. For example, **intdiv(10,3)** returns **3**.

Making comparisons

The operators that are commonly used in PHP scripts to compare two values are listed in the table below:

Operator:	Comparative test:
==	Equality
===	Identicality
!==	Non-identicality
!= \<>	Inequality
>	Greater than
<	Less than
>=	Greater than or equal to
<=	Less than or equal to
\<=>	Spaceship

The == equality operator compares two operands and returns a Boolean **TRUE** result if both are numerically equal in value, otherwise it returns **FALSE**. Characters and strings are also compared numerically by their ASCII code value. Conversely, the != inequality operator returns **TRUE** if the two operands are <u>not</u> equal, otherwise it returns **FALSE**.

The > "greater than" operator compares two operands and returns **TRUE** if the first is greater in value than the second, or it returns **FALSE** if it is equal or less in value. The < "less than" operator makes the same comparison but returns **TRUE** if the first operand is less in value than the second, otherwise it returns **FALSE**. Adding the = operator after a > "greater than" or < "less than" operator makes it also return **TRUE** when the two operands are exactly equal.

The \<=> spaceship operator returns an integer value of 1 when the first operand is greater than the second, -1 when the first operand is less than the second, or 0 when the operands are equal.

The PHP **var_dump()** function can be used to see the type and value resulting from each kind of comparison.

The \<=> spaceship operator is a new feature in PHP 7.

Hot tip

Equality and inequality operators are useful in testing the state of two variables to perform conditional branching in a PHP script.

1 Create a valid HTML document, like the one listed on page 16, then insert PHP tags into the body section

```php
<?php
    # Statements to be inserted here.
?>
```

comparison.php

2 Now, insert statements between the PHP tags to create and initialize five variables

```php
$zero = 0 ; $nil = 0 ; $one = 1 ; $upr = 'A' ; $lwr = 'a' ;
```

3 Next, insert statements to display equality comparisons

```php
echo "0 == 0 : " ;       var_dump( $zero == $nil ) ;
echo "<br>0 == 1 : " ;   var_dump( $zero == $one ) ;
echo "<br>A == a : " ;   var_dump( $upr == $lwr ) ;
echo "<br>A != a : " ;   var_dump( $upr == $lwr ) ;
```

Hot tip

The ASCII code value for uppercase 'A' is 65 and for lowercase 'a' it's 97 – so their comparison here returns **FALSE**.

4 Insert statements to display comparison evaluations

```php
echo "<hr>1 > 0 : " ;      var_dump( $one > $nil ) ;
echo "<br>0 >= 0 : " ;     var_dump( $zero >= $nil ) ;
echo "<br>1 <= 0 : " ;     var_dump( $one <= $nil ) ;
echo "<hr>1 <=> 0 : " ;    var_dump( $one <=> $nil ) ;
echo "<br>1 <=> 1 : " ;    var_dump( $one <=> $one ) ;
echo "<br>0 <=> 1 : " ;    var_dump( $nil <=> $one ) ;
```

5 Save the document in your web server's **/htdocs** directory as **comparison.php** then open the page via HTTP to see the results get displayed

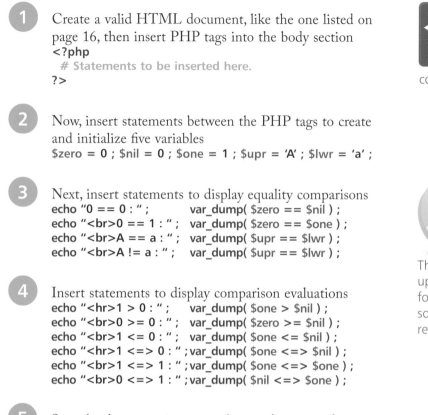

Hot tip

A Boolean **TRUE** value is represented numerically by 1 in PHP language.

Examining conditions

Conditional operator

The conditional operator **?:** is also known as the "ternary" operator as it has three components. This operator first evaluates an expression for a **TRUE** or **FALSE** Boolean value, then returns one of two specified results depending on the evaluation. The conditional operator syntax looks like this:

(*test-expression*) ? *result-if-true* : *result-if-false* ;

The conditional operator can be used to evaluate whether a given number is one or more, to ensure correct grammar in output regarding singular and plural items. This avoids awkward phrases such as "There is 5":

$verb = ($number == 1) ? 'is' : 'are ';
echo "There $verb $number" ;

In this case, when the **$number** variable has a value of one, the 'is' result will be assigned to the **$verb** variable, otherwise the 'are' result will be assigned.

The conditional operator can also be used to evaluate whether a given number is odd or even ("parity") by examining if there is any remainder after dividing the number by two, then assign an appropriate string result like this:

$parity = ($number % 2 == 0) ? 'Odd' : 'Even' ;
echo "$number is $parity" ;

In this case, when the modulus operation returns a value of one, the 'Odd' result will be assigned to the **$parity** variable, otherwise the 'Even' result will be assigned.

Null coalescing operator

PHP has a special **NULL** value that is a built-in constant, which represents a variable with no value whatsoever – not even zero. Variables that have not been assigned a value will evaluate as **NULL**. The snappily named **??** "null coalescing" operator can be used to traverse a number of operands, from left to right, and return the value of the first operand that is not **NULL**. If none of the operands have a value (and are not **NULL**) then the null coalescing operator will itself return a **NULL** result.

Beware

Do not use more than one **?:** conditional operator in a single statement as the results may be unpredictable.

The **??** null coalescing operator is a new feature in PHP 7.

...cont'd

1 Create a valid HTML document, like the one listed on page 16, then insert PHP tags into the body section
```php
<?php
  # Statements to be inserted here.
?>
```

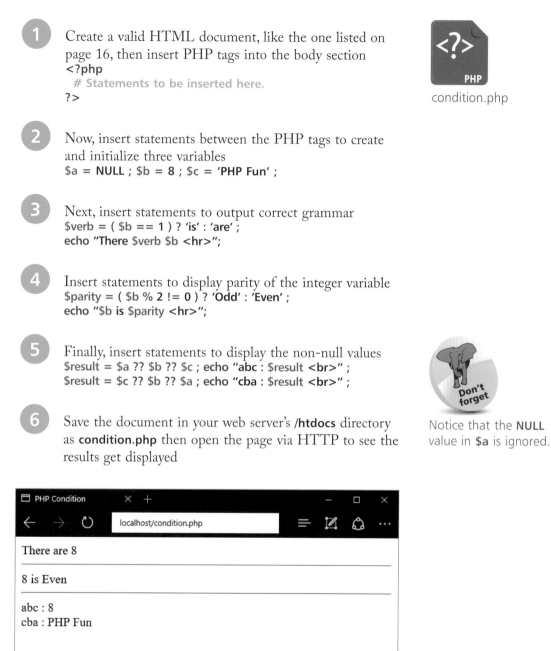

PHP

condition.php

2 Now, insert statements between the PHP tags to create and initialize three variables
```php
$a = NULL ; $b = 8 ; $c = 'PHP Fun' ;
```

3 Next, insert statements to output correct grammar
```php
$verb = ( $b == 1 ) ? 'is' : 'are' ;
echo "There $verb $b <hr>";
```

4 Insert statements to display parity of the integer variable
```php
$parity = ( $b % 2 != 0 ) ? 'Odd' : 'Even' ;
echo "$b is $parity <hr>";
```

5 Finally, insert statements to display the non-null values
```php
$result = $a ?? $b ?? $c ; echo "abc : $result <br>" ;
$result = $c ?? $b ?? $a ; echo "cba : $result <br>" ;
```

Don't forget

Notice that the **NULL** value in **$a** is ignored.

6 Save the document in your web server's **/htdocs** directory as **condition.php** then open the page via HTTP to see the results get displayed

| PHP Condition | × | + | — | □ | × |

← → ○ localhost/condition.php

There are 8

---

8 is Even

---

abc : 8
cba : PHP Fun

Assessing logic

The logical operators most commonly used in PHP scripts are listed in the table below:

Operator:		Operation:
and	&&	Logical AND
or	||	Logical OR
xor		Logical eXclusive OR
!		Logical NOT

Hot tip

The **&&** operator is an alternative form of the **and** operator. Similarly, the **||** operator is an alternative form of the **or** operator.

Hot tip

The term "Boolean" refers to a system of logical thought developed by the English mathematician George Boole (1815-1864).

The logical operators are used with operands that have the Boolean values of **TRUE** or **FALSE**, or an expression that can convert to **TRUE** or **FALSE**.

The **and** operator will evaluate two operands and return **TRUE**, only if both operands are themselves **TRUE**. Otherwise the **and** operator will return **FALSE**. This is used in conditional branching where the direction of a PHP script is determined by testing two conditions. If both conditions are satisfied the script will go in a certain direction, otherwise it will take a different direction.

Unlike the **and** operator that needs both operands to be **TRUE** the **or** operator will evaluate two operands and return **TRUE** if either one of the operands is itself **TRUE**. If neither operand is **TRUE** then the **or** operator will return **FALSE**. This is useful to perform an action if either one of two test conditions has been met.

The **xor** operator will evaluate two operands and only return **TRUE** if either one of the operands is itself **TRUE** – but not both. If neither operand is **TRUE**, or if both operands are **TRUE**, the **xor** operator will return **FALSE**.

The ! logical NOT operator is a "unary" operator – that is used before a single operand. It returns the inverse value of the given operand, so if the variable **$var** is a **TRUE** value then ! **$var** would return a **FALSE** value. The ! operator is useful to toggle the value of a variable in a loop with a statement like $var = ! $var. On each iteration the value is reversed, like flicking a switch on and off.

1 Create a valid HTML document, like the one listed on page 16, then insert PHP tags into the body section
```
<?php
    # Statements to be inserted here.
?>
```

logic.php

2 Now, insert between the PHP tags statements to create and initialize two variables with Boolean values
```
$yes = TRUE ; $no = FALSE ;
```

3 Next, insert statements to display AND evaluations
```
$result = ( $no && $no ) ? 'TRUE' : 'FALSE' ;
        echo "No AND No returns $result <br>" ;
$result = ( $yes && $no ) ? 'TRUE' : 'FALSE'  ;
        echo "Yes AND No returns : $result <br>" ;
$result = ( $yes && $yes ) ? 'TRUE' : 'FALSE'  ;
        echo "Yes AND Yes returns $result <hr>" ;
```

Hot tip

PHP also has an **XOR** (exclusive **OR**) operator that performs the equivalent evaluation of **AND NOT** together.

4 Insert statements to display OR and NOT evaluations
```
$result = ( $no || $no ) ? 'TRUE' : 'FALSE'  ;
        echo "No OR No returns $result <br>" ;
$result = ( $yes || $no ) ? 'TRUE' : 'FALSE'  ;
        echo "Yes OR No returns $result <br>" ;
$result = ( $yes || $yes ) ? 'TRUE' : 'FALSE'  ;
        echo "Yes OR Yes returns $result <hr>" ;
$result = ( ! $yes ) ? 'TRUE' : 'FALSE'  ;
        echo "NOT Yes returns $result <br>" ;
```

5 Save the document in your web server's **/htdocs** directory as **logic.php** then open the page via HTTP to see the results get displayed

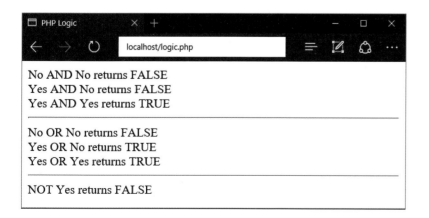

No AND No returns FALSE
Yes AND No returns FALSE
Yes AND Yes returns TRUE

No OR No returns FALSE
Yes OR No returns TRUE
Yes OR Yes returns TRUE

NOT Yes returns FALSE

Don't forget

Notice that evaluation of **FALSE && FALSE** returns **FALSE** – maybe demonstrating the anecdote "two wrongs don't make a right".

Many PHP programmers never use bitwise operators, but it is useful to understand what they are and how they may be used.

Comparing bits

A byte comprises eight bits that can each contain a **1** or a **0** to store a binary number, representing decimal values from 0 to 255. Each bit contributes a decimal component only when that bit contains a **1**. Components are designated right-to-left from the "Least Significant Bit" (LSB) to the "Most Significant Bit" (MSB). The binary number in the bit pattern below represents decimal 50.

Bit No.	8 MSB	7	6	5	4	3	2	1 LSB
Decimal	128	64	32	16	8	4	2	1
Binary	0	0	1	1	0	0	1	0

It is possible to manipulate individual parts of a byte using "bitwise" operators. Bitwise operators allow evaluation and manipulation of specific bits within an integer.

Each half of a byte is known as a "nibble" (4 bits). The binary numbers in the examples in the table describe values stored in a nibble.

Operator:	Name:	Binary number operation:
|	OR	Return a **1** in each bit where either of two compared bits is a **1** Example: **1010 | 0101 = 1111**
&	AND	Return a **1** in each bit where both of two compared bits is a **1** Example: **1010 && 1100 = 1000**
~	NOT	Return a **1** in each bit where neither of two compared bits is a **1** Example: **1010 ~ 0011 = 0100**
^	XOR	Return a **1** in each bit where only one of two compared bits is a **1** Example: **1010 ^ 0100 = 1110**
<<	Shift left	Move each bit that is a **1** a specified number of bits to the left Example: **0010 << 2 = 1000**
>>	Shift right	Move each bit that is a **1** a specified number of bits to the right Example: **1000 >> 2 = 0010**

Unless programming for a device with limited resources, there is seldom a need to utilize bitwise operators, but they can be useful. For instance, the ^ (eXclusive OR) operator lets you exchange values between two variables without the need for a third variable:

1. Create a valid HTML document, like the one listed on page 16, then insert PHP tags into the body section
```
<?php
   # Statements to be inserted here.
?>
```

bitwise.php

2. Now, insert between the PHP tags statements to create and initialize two variables with integer values
```
$x = 5 ; $y =10 ;
```

3. Next, add a statement to display the assigned values
```
echo "X : $x , Y : $y <br>" ;
```

4. Insert three XOR statements to exchange the variable values by binary bit manipulation
```
$x = $x ^ $y ; /* 1010 ^ 0101 = 1111 (decimal 15) */
$y = $x ^ $y ; /* 1111 ^ 0101 = 1010 (decimal 10) */
$x = $x ^ $y ; /* 1111 ^ 1010 = 0101 (decimal 5)  */
```

5. Finally, add a statement to display the manipulated values
```
echo "X : $x , Y : $y <br>" ;
```

6. Save the document in your web server's **/htdocs** directory as **bitwise.php** then open the page via HTTP to see the XOR bitwise magic

Beware

Do not confuse bitwise operators with logical operators. Bitwise operators compare binary numbers, whereas logical operators evaluate Boolean values.

Changing values

The PHP ++ increment operator and -- decrement operator alter the given number by one and return the resulting new value. These are most often used to count iterations in a loop. The increment operator increases the value by one and the decrement operator decreases the value by one. Each of these operators may appear either before or after the variable containing the number to be changed – to different effect! When either of these operators are placed before the variable ("prefixed"), they change the value by one then return the modified value, but when they are placed after the variable ("postfixed") they return the current value, then change the value by one:

change.php

1. Create a valid HTML document, like the one listed on page 16, then insert PHP tags into the body section
```
<?php
    # Statements to be inserted here.
?>
```

2. Now, insert between the PHP tags statements to create and initialize four variables with the same integer value
```
$a = $b = $c = $d = 5 ;
```

3. Next, add statements to change each of the values by one and display the new integers
```
echo "++A : ". ++$a . "<br>--B : ". --$b ."<hr>" ;
echo "C++ : ". $c++ . "[now C : ". $c ."]<br>" ;
echo "D-- : ". $d-- . "[now D : ". $d ."]<br>" ;
```

Hot tip

Notice how the . concatenation operator is used here to form strings. You can also use the .= concatenating assignment operator to append one string onto another string.

4. Save the document in your web server's **/htdocs** directory as **change.php** then open the page via HTTP to see the results

PHP Inc/Decrement   ×   +

localhost/change.php

++A : 6
--B : 4
_____

C++ : 5 [now C : 6]
D-- : 5 [now D : 4]

Grasping precedence

PHP operator precedence determines how expressions are grouped for evaluation. For example, the expression **1 + 5 * 3** evaluates to 16, not 18, because the ***** multiplication operator has a higher precedence than the **+** addition operator. Parentheses can be used to specify precedence, so that **(1 + 5) * 3** evaluates to 18. When operators have equal precedence their "associativity" determines how expressions are grouped. For example, the - subtraction operator is left-associative, so **8 - 4 - 2** is grouped as **(8 - 4) - 2** and evaluates to 2. The table below lists common operators in order of precedence, with the highest-precedence ones at the top. Operators on the same line have equal precedence, so operator associativity determines how expressions are grouped.

Operator:	Associativity:	
**		Right
++ -- ~		Right
!		Right
* / %	Left	
+ - .	Left	
<< >>	Left	
< <= > >=		None
== != === !== <> <=>		None
&	Left	
^	Left	
|	Left	
&&	Left	
||	Left	
??		Right
?=	Left	
= += -= *= /= **= .= %= &= |= ^= <<= >>= =>		Right
and	Left	
xor	Left	
or	Left	
,	Left	

Beware

The eagle-eyed will notice that the alternative forms of logical operators have different levels of precedence. This can cause unexpected results in an expression such as **$bool = true and false** versus the alternative **$bool = true && false**. Try each of these then do **var_dump($bool)** to see the difference.

Summary

- Arithmetical operators can form expressions with operands for addition **+**, subtraction **-**, multiplication *****, division **/**, modulus **%**, and exponentiation ******

- The assignment operator **=** can be combined with any arithmetical operator to perform an arithmetical calculation then assign the result

- Comparison operators can form expressions with operands for equality **==**, inequality **!=**, identicality or not **===**, **!==**, greater **>**, less **<**, greater, less or equal **>=**, **<=**, **<=>**

- The conditional operator **?:** evaluates an expression for a **TRUE** or **FALSE** Boolean value, then returns one of two specified results depending on the evaluation

- The **??** null coalescing operator traverses operands from left to right and returns the first value that is not null

- Logical operators **and**, **&&**, **or**, **||** and **xor** form expressions evaluating two operands and return a value of true or false

- The logical **!** not operator returns the inverse Boolean value of a single operand

- Bitwise operators **|**, **&**, **~**, **^**, **<<** and **>>** allow the evaluation and manipulation of specific bits within an integer

- Increment **++** or decrement **--** operators that prefix a variable change its value by one and return the result

- Increment **++** or decrement **--** operators that postfix a variable return its current value, then change its value by one

- Operator precedence determines how expressions are grouped for evaluation

- When operators have equal precedence, their associativity determines how the expression is grouped for evaluation

- The **var_dump()** function can be used to see the type and value resulting from an expression

- The special **NULL** constant represents a variable that has no value whatsoever, not even zero

4 Testing conditions

This chapter demonstrates the various PHP control structures that determine how a script will proceed.

The **if** construct is one of the most important features in PHP, and in most other programming languages.

54

When the code to be executed is just a single statement, the braces may optionally be omitted, but you may prefer to always include the braces for consistency.

Seeking truth

The **if** keyword is used to perform the basic conditional test that evaluates a given expression for a Boolean value of **TRUE** or **FALSE**. Statements within braces following the evaluation will only be executed when the expression is found to be **TRUE**. When the expression is found to be **FALSE**, the PHP parser simply moves on to the next part of the script.

The syntax of an **if** conditional test statement looks like this:

if (*test-expression*) { *statement-to-execute-when-true* ; }

There may be multiple statements to be executed when the test is **TRUE** but each statement must be terminated by a semi-colon:

```
if ( test-expression )
{
        statement-to-execute-when-true ;
        statement-to-execute-when-true ;
        statement-to-execute-when-true ;
}
```

Multiple expressions can be tested using the logical **&&** or **and** operator to ensure that following statements will only be executed when both expressions are found to be **TRUE**, like this:

```
if ( ( test-expression ) && ( test-expression ) )
{
        statement-to-execute-when-true ;
        statement-to-execute-when-true ;
        statement-to-execute-when-true ;
}
```

Alternatively, **if** conditional test statements can be nested to test multiple expressions so that statements will only be executed when all tests are found to be **TRUE**, like this:

```
if ( test-expression )
{
        if ( test-expression )
        {
                statement-to-execute-when-true ;
                statement-to-execute-when-true ;
                statement-to-execute-when-true ;
        }
}
```

Multiple **if** conditional test statements can be made to provide alternatives for the script to follow.

1 Between PHP tags, begin a script with a statement that initializes an integer variable
```
<?php
$num = 8 ;
```

if.php

2 Next, add statements that output a result when a conditional test of numerical size is found to be **TRUE**
```
if ( $num > 5 ) { echo "$num exceeds 5<br>" ; }
if ( $num <= 5 ) { echo "$num is below 6<br>" ; }
```

3 Now, add statements that output a result when a conditional test of parity is found to be **TRUE**
```
if ( $num % 2 == 0 ) { echo "$num is Even<br>" ; }
if ( $num % 2 != 0 ) { echo "$num is Odd<br>" ; }
?>
```

4 Save the document in your web server's **/htdocs** directory as **if.php** then open the page via HTTP to see the results from successful tests get displayed

PHP Conditional If	×	+	—	□	×
← → ↺	localhost/if.php		≡ 🖊 ◌	...	

8 exceeds 5
8 is Even

5 Edit the integer variable then save the modified script and refresh the browser to see the results from other successful tests get displayed
```
$num = 3 ;
```

PHP Conditional If	×	+	—	□	×
← → ↺	localhost/if.php		≡ 🖊 ◌	...	

3 is below 6
3 is Odd

Don't forget

When the tested condition is **FALSE**, the PHP parser ignores its statement block and simply moves on.

Providing alternatives

It is often preferable to extend an **if** statement by appending an **else** statement, specifying statements within braces to be executed when the expressions evaluated by the **if** statement are found to be **FALSE**, with this syntax:

```
if ( test-expression )
{
        statement-to-execute-when-true ;
        statement-to-execute-when-true ;
        statement-to-execute-when-true ;
}
else
{
        statement-to-execute-when-false ;
        statement-to-execute-when-false ;
        statement-to-execute-when-false ;
}
```

Alternative expressions may also be evaluated in a conditional test by adding an **elseif** statement, specifying statements within braces to be executed when the alternative expression is found to be **TRUE**. An **else** statement can be appended here too, to specify statements within braces to be executed when the expressions evaluated by the **if** and **elseif** statements are found to be **FALSE**, with this syntax:

```
if ( test-expression )
{
        statement-to-execute-when-true ;
        statement-to-execute-when-true ;
        statement-to-execute-when-true ;
}
elseif ( test-expression )
{
        statement-to-execute-when-true ;
        statement-to-execute-when-true ;
        statement-to-execute-when-true ;
}
else
{
        statement-to-execute-when-false ;
        statement-to-execute-when-false ;
        statement-to-execute-when-false ;
}
```

This is a fundamental programming technique that offers the script different directions in which to proceed, depending on the result of the evaluations, and is known as "conditional branching".

Hot tip

The **elseif** keyword can also be written as two separate words: **else if**.

Beware

You may come across some PHP scripts that use a **:** colon character rather than curly brackets. This is not recommended as **if** and **else if** will only be considered exactly the same when using curly brackets.

56

1 Between PHP tags, begin a script with a statement that outputs a result only when a tested expression is **TRUE**

```php
<?php
if ( 4 > 2 ) { echo '<p>Yes, 4 is greater than 2 <br>' ; }
```

else.php

2 Next, add a statement that outputs a result only when two tested expressions are both found to be **TRUE**

```php
if ( ( 4 > 2 ) && ( 8 > 4 ) )
{ echo '4 is greater than 2 AND 8 is greater than 4<br>' ; }
```

3 Now, add a statement that outputs a result when a tested expression is found to be **TRUE** or **FALSE**

```php
if ( 4 > 8 )
{ echo '4 is greater than 8 <br>' ; }
else
{ echo '4 is less than 8 <br>' ; }
```

4 Finally, add a statement that outputs a result when either of two tested expressions are found to be **TRUE** or when both tested expressions are found to be **FALSE**

```php
if ( 4 > 8 )
{ echo 'This test is True </p>' ; }
elseif ( 8 > 4 )
{ echo 'Alternative test is True </p>' ; }
else
{ echo 'Both tests are False </p>' ; }
?>
```

5 Save the document in your web server's **/htdocs** directory as **else.php** then open the page via HTTP to see the results of conditional branching get displayed

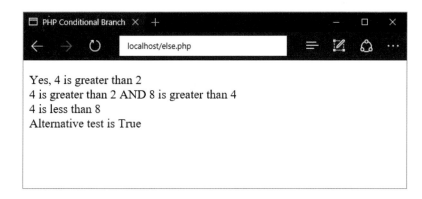

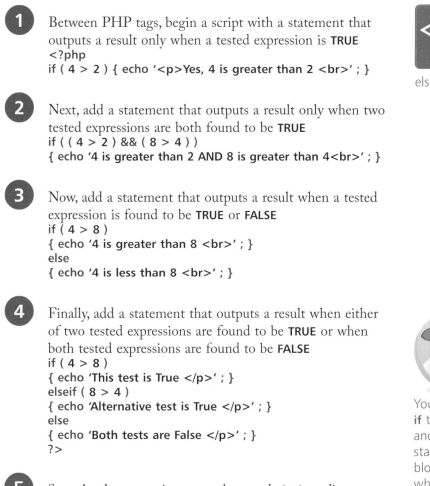

You can nest conditional **if** tests (one inside another) so that statements in the inner block only get executed when both tests are found to be **TRUE**.

57

Switching branches

Conditional branching performed by multiple **if-elseif-else** statements can often be performed more efficiently by a **switch** statement when the test expression just evaluates one condition.

The **switch** statement works in an unusual way. It takes a given value as its parameter argument then seeks to match that value from a number of **case** statements. Code to be executed when a match is found is included in each **case** statement.

It is important to end each **case** statement with a **break** keyword statement, so the **switch** statement will then exit when a match is found without seeking further matches – unless that is the deliberate requirement.

Optionally, the list of **case** statements can be followed by a single final **default** statement to specify code to be executed in the event that no matches are found within any of the **case** statements. So the syntax of a switch statement typically looks like this:

```
switch ( test-value )
{
  case match-value : statements-to-execute-when-matched ; break ;
  case match-value : statements-to-execute-when-matched ; break ;
  case match-value : statements-to-execute-when-matched ; break ;
  default : statements-to-execute-when-no-match-found ;
}
```

A **switch** statement can have many **case** statements, but no two of its **case** statements can attempt to match the same value.

Where a number of match-values are to each execute the same statements, only the final **case** statement need include the statements to be executed and the **break** statement to exit the **switch** statement block. For example, to output the same message for match-values of 0, 1 and 2:

```
switch ( $number )
{
  case 0 :
  case 1 :
  case 2 : echo 'Less than 3' ; break ;
  case 3 : echo 'Exactly 3' ; break ;
  default : echo 'Greater than 3 or less than zero' ;
}
```

58

1 Between PHP tags, begin a script with statements that initialize two variables with an integer and character value

```php
<?php
$number = 2 ; $letter = 'B' ;
```

switch.php

2 Next, add a **switch** statement to match the integer value

```php
switch ( $number )
{
  case 1 : echo 'Number is One<br>' ; break ;
  case 2 : echo 'Number is Two<br>' ; break ;
  case 3 : echo 'Number is Three<br>' ; break ;
  default : echo 'Number is Unrecognized<br>' ;
}
```

3 Now, add a **switch** statement to match the character value

```php
switch ( $letter )
{
  case 'A' : echo 'Letter is A<br>' ; break ;
  case 'B' : echo 'Letter is B<br>' ; break ;
  case 'C' : echo 'Letter is C<br>' ; break ;
  default : echo 'Letter is Unrecognized<br>' ;
}
```

4 Finally, add a **switch** statement to match against multiple integer values

```php
switch ( $number )
{
  case 0 : case 1 : case 2 : echo 'Less than 3<br>' ; break ;
  default : echo '3 or more, or less than zero' ;
}
?>
```

Hot tip

In **switch** statements, the **case** keyword, match-value and colon character are regarded as a unique "label".

5 Save the document in your web server's **/htdocs** directory as **switch.php** then open the page via HTTP to see the results of conditional branching get displayed

PHP Switch Branching

localhost/switch.php

Number is Two
Letter is B
Less than 3

Performing loops

A loop is a piece of code in a script that automatically repeats. One complete execution of all statements within a loop is called an "iteration", or a "pass". The length of a loop is controlled by a conditional test made within the loop. While the tested expression is found to be **TRUE** the loop will continue – until the tested expression is found to be **FALSE** at which point the loop ends.

In PHP there are four types of loop structure:

- **for** loop – performs a specified number of iterations

- **while** loop – performs iterations only while a test made at the start of each iteration evaluates as **TRUE**

- **do while** loop – performs iterations only while a test made at the end of each iteration evaluates as **TRUE**

- **foreach** loop – performs iterations to traverse each element of an array, as introduced on page 26

Perhaps the most interesting loop structure is the **for** loop, which typically has this syntax:

```
for ( initializer ; test-expression ; updater )
{
        statement-to-execute-when-true ;
        statement-to-execute-when-true ;
        statement-to-execute-when-true ;
}
```

The initializer is used to set a starting value for a counter of the number of iterations made by the loop. An integer variable is used for this purpose and is traditionally named "i".

Upon each iteration of the loop, the test-expression is evaluated and that iteration will only continue while this expression is **TRUE**. When the test-expression becomes **FALSE**, the loop ends immediately without executing the statements again. With every iteration the counter is updated then the statements executed.

Loops can be nested, one within another, to allow complete execution of all iterations of an inner nested loop on each iteration of the outer loop.

Hot tip

The updater may be an incrementer, or it may be a decrementer in a loop that counts down rather than counting up.

1 Between PHP tags, create a script with a **for** loop to output the loop counter value on each of three iterations

```php
<?php
for ( $i = 1 ; $i < 4 ; $i++ )
{
  echo "<dt>Outer loop iteration $i" ;

  # Nested loop to be inserted here.
}
?>
```

forloop.php

2 Save the document in your web server's **/htdocs** directory as **forloop.php** then open the page via HTTP to see the loop counter values get displayed

3 Now, insert a nested **for** loop to output its loop counter value in a list on each of three iterations

```php
for ( $j = 1 ; $j < 4 ; $j++ )
{
  echo "<dd>Inner loop iteration $j" ;
}
```

4 Save the document once more then open the page via HTTP to see both loop counter values get displayed

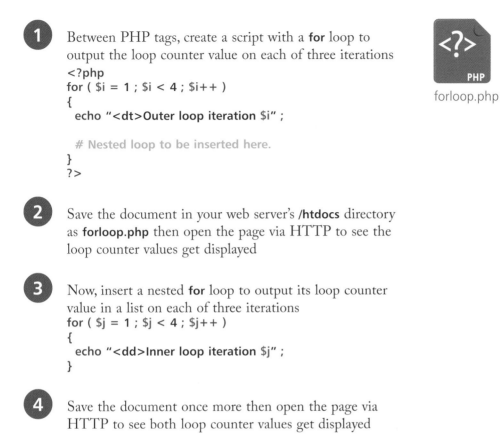

A **for** loop counter can also count down – by decrementing the counter value on each iteration using **$i--** in place of **$i++**.

61

Ensure that the test expression in a loop structure will at some point become **FALSE** to avoid creating an infinite loop that never ends.

62

Hot tip

You will discover later in this book how a PHP while loop is used to retrieve records from a MySQL database.

Looping while true

A **while** loop is an alternative to the **for** loop described in the previous example. The **while** loop also requires an initializer, test-expression, and an updater, but these are not neatly listed within a single pair of parentheses as they are in a **for** loop. Instead the initializer must appear before the start of the loop block, and the test-expression must appear within parentheses after the **while** keyword, followed by braces containing both an updater and the statements to be executed on each iteration.

initializer
while (*test-expression* **)**
{
      statement/s-to-be-executed ;
      updater ;
}

A **do while** loop provides a subtle variation on the syntax above by placing the **do** keyword before the loop block and moving the **while** statement to after the loop block:

initializer
do {
      statement/s-to-be-executed ;
      updater ;
}
while (*test-expression* **) ;**

Both **while** loops and **do while** loops will proceed to make iterations until the test-expression is found to be **FALSE**, at which point the loop will exit. It is therefore essential that the loop body contains code that will, at some point, change the result of the test-expression evaluation – otherwise an infinite loop is created which will lock the system. The significant difference between a **while** loop and a **do while** loop is that a **while** loop will not make a single iteration if the test-expression is **FALSE** on its first evaluation. In contrast, a **do while** loop will always make at least one iteration because its statements are executed before the evaluation is made. If this is desirable a **do while** loop is obviously the best choice, otherwise the choice between a **for** loop and a **while** loop is largely a matter of personal preference. One rule of thumb suggests that a **for** loop is best used to perform a specific number of iterations, whereas a **while** loop is best used to iterate until a certain condition is met. Loops are the perfect partner to use with arrays as each iteration can effortlessly read or write into successive array elements.

1 Between PHP tags, begin a script with a statement to create an array

```php
<?php
$numbers = array( 10 , 20 , 30 ) ;
```

whileloop.php

2 Next, add a **while** loop to output the value of each array element

```php
echo '<dt>While Loop : ' ;
$i = 0 ;
while ( $i < 3 )
{
  echo "<dd>Element $i = $numbers[$i] " ;
  $i++ ;
}
```

3 Now, add a **do while** loop to output the value of each array element

```php
echo '<dt>Do While Loop : ' ;
$i = 0 ;
do
{
  echo "<dd>Element $i = $numbers[$i] " ;
  $i++ ;
}
while ( $i < 3 ) ;
?>
```

4 Save the document in your web server's **/htdocs** directory as **whileloop.php** then open the page via HTTP to see the array element values get identically displayed

Change the value in this test expression to zero – so **while ($i = 0)** in both loops – to see only the first iteration of the **do while** loop get executed.

Breaking from loops

The **break** keyword can be used to prematurely terminate a loop when a specified condition is met. The **break** statement is situated inside the loop statement block and is preceded by a test expression. When the test returns **TRUE**, the loop ends immediately and the program proceeds on to the next task. For example, in a nested inner loop it proceeds to the next iteration of the outer loop.

breakcontinue.php

 1 Between PHP tags, begin a script with a **for** loop that performs three iterations
```php
<?php
for ( $i = 1 ; $i < 4 ; $i++ )
{
    # Nested loop to be inserted here (step 2).
}
```

2 Next, insert a nested **for** loop that also performs three iterations
```php
for ( $j = 1 ; $j < 4 ; $j++ )
{
    # Statements to be inserted here (steps 5 & 6).
}
?>
```

3 Now, insert a statement that outputs the value of both loop counters on each iteration
```php
echo "Running i = $i and j = $j <br>" ;
```

4 Save the document in your web server's **/htdocs** directory as **breakcontinue.php** then open the page via HTTP to see both loop counter values get displayed

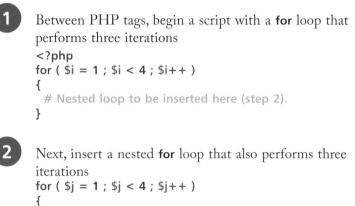

```
PHP Breaking Loops    ×   +                          —  □  ×

←  →  ↻        localhost/breakcontinue.php        ≡  ▨  ◌  ...

Running i = 1 and j = 1
Running i = 1 and j = 2
Running i = 1 and j = 3
Running i = 2 and j = 1
Running i = 2 and j = 2
Running i = 2 and j = 3
Running i = 3 and j = 1
Running i = 3 and j = 2
Running i = 3 and j = 3
```

5 Next, insert this **break** statement at the very beginning of the inner loop block, to break out of the inner loop – then save the document and view the change

```php
if ( $i == 2 && $j == 1 )
{
  echo "Breaks inner loop when i = $i and j = $j <br>" ;
  break ;
}
```

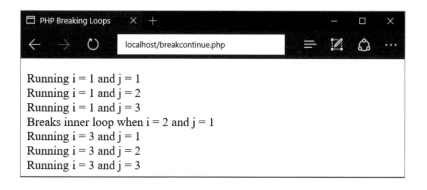

The **continue** keyword can be used to skip a single iteration of a loop when a specified condition is met. The **continue** statement is situated inside the loop statement block and is preceded by a test expression. When the test returns **TRUE** that single iteration ends.

6 Now, insert this **continue** statement at the beginning of the inner loop block, to skip the first iteration of the inner loop – then save the document and view the change

```php
if ( $i == 1 && $j == 1 )
{
  echo "Continues inner loop when i = $i and j = $j <br>" ;
  continue ;
}
```

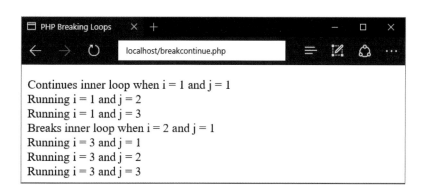

Here, the **break** statement halts all three iterations of the inner loop when the outer loop tries to run it the second time.

Here, the **continue** statement just skips the first iteration of the inner loop when the outer loop tries to run it for the first time.

Summary

- The **if** keyword performs the basic conditional test that evaluates an expression for a Boolean value of **TRUE** or **FALSE**

- Statements within braces following the evaluation will only be executed when the expression is found **TRUE**

- Multiple expressions can be tested using the logical **&&** operator, or by nesting multiple **if** conditional tests

- The **else** keyword specifies statements to be executed when the expression evaluated by the **if** statement is found **FALSE**

- The **elseif** keyword is used to append an alternative expression to be evaluated and statements to be executed when **TRUE**

- Multiple **if-elseif-else** statements can often be performed more efficiently by a **switch** statement

- The **case** keyword is used to specify a value to be matched in a **switch** statement block

- Each **case** statement must end with a **break** keyword statement so the **switch** will exit when a match is found

- A **default** statement specifies code to be executed in the event that no matches are found within any **case** statements

- A loop is a piece of code in a script that automatically repeats until a test expression becomes **FALSE**

- The PHP loop structures are **for, while, do while** and **foreach**

- A **for** loop structure specifies an initializer, a test expression and an updater that increments (or decrements) a counter

- An updater must always be included in the statement block of a **while** loop and a **do while** loop

- Unlike a **while** loop, a **do while** loop will always execute its statements at least once

- The **break** keyword can be used to prematurely terminate a loop when a specified condition is met

- The **continue** keyword can be used to skip a single iteration of a loop when a specified condition is met

5 Employing functions

This chapter demonstrates how to create re-usable blocks of code in functions.

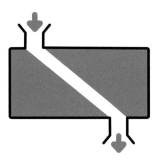

Defining functions

PHP provides many built-in functions that can be called by name in your scripts to execute pre-defined actions, such as the array sorting functions described on page 28. Additionally, you may create your own custom functions to execute specified actions when called. This usefully allows PHP scripts to be modularized into sections of code that are easier to understand and maintain.

Your custom function names may contain any combination of letters, numbers and the underscore character, but must begin with a letter or an underscore. Understandably, to avoid conflict the name may not duplicate an existing built-in function name, so for example you may not create a custom function named "sort".

Unlike PHP variables, function names are case-insensitive so **cube()**, **Cube()** and **CUBE()** can all reference the same function. Nonetheless,- it is recommended you always use the same case as that used to name the function in the function definition.

A function definition is created in a PHP script simply by stating its name after the **function** keyword, followed by parentheses and curly brackets (braces) containing the statements to be executed each time that function gets called:

Don't forget

PHP variable names are case-sensitive, but PHP function names are not.

```
function function_name ( )
{
  statement-to-be-executed ;
  statement-to-be-executed ;
  statement-to-be-executed ;
}
```

A PHP script can then call upon a defined function by name using **function_name( );** to execute the statements it contains whenever required. Although the interpreter runs the script from top to bottom, a function call can appear before the function definition. This is not good programming practice, however, so you should define functions before they are called.

Functions may contain any valid PHP script code and may even contain a further function definition. In that case, the inner function will not exist until the outer function has been called.

1 Begin a PHP script with a statement to define a function

```php
<?php
function greet()
{
  echo 'Hello User!<br>' ;
}
```

function.php

2 Next, add a statement to call the function defined in the previous step, to have it execute its statement

```php
greet() ;
```

3 Now, define another function that contains an inner function definition and a further statement

```php
function outer()
{
  function inner()
  {
    echo 'Inner function called.<br>' ;
  }
  echo 'Inner function created.<br>' ;
}
```

4 Finally, add statements to call each of the functions defined in the previous step

```php
outer() ;
inner() ;
?>
```

5 Save the document in your web server's **/htdocs** directory as **function.php** then open the page via HTTP to see the output from each function call

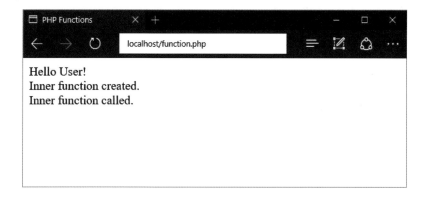

```
Hello User!
Inner function created.
Inner function called.
```

Hot tip

Remove the call to the outer function to see an undefined function error when the script attempts to call the inner function.

Parameters must be specified in the function declaration as a comma-separated list, and argument values passed by the caller as a comma-separated list.

The ability to specify argument data types is a new feature in PHP 7.

Passing arguments

Data can be passed to functions as "arguments" in the same way you can pass arguments to some built-in PHP functions. For example, the **sort()** function takes the array to be sorted as its argument. Functions can be created with any number of arguments but when called, data must be supplied for each argument to avoid an error.

A function accepting arguments is defined by including a comma-separated list of "parameters" within the parentheses after the function name, like this:

```
function function_name ( $arg_1 , $arg_2 , $arg_3 )
{
    statement-to-be-executed ;
    statement-to-be-executed ;
    statement-to-be-executed ;
}
```

Parameter names must adhere to the same naming conventions required for PHP variables and should ideally be meaningful, to represent the nature of the data they will be passed. The argument data must be passed by the call in the correct order and can then be used by the statements within that function.

Optionally, the function definition can specify the type of data to be passed from the caller by including a type description before the parameter name. Valid type descriptions include **int, float, string, bool, callable** and **array**. When types are specified, a call that attempts to pass an incorrect data type to the function will result in an error.

It is important to recognize that by default, argument data is passed "by value". This means that if a function call specifies a variable name, only a copy of the data within that variable gets passed to the function. Modifying the argument will not affect the original data stored in the variable when it is passed by value.

If you want a function to modify data stored in a variable, specified in a function call, you must pass it "by reference". This allows the function to operate directly on the original data. Modifying the argument will affect the original data in the variable when it is passed by reference. To ensure that an argument is always passed to a function by reference, you need simply prefix an **&** ampersand before the parameter name in the function definition.

1. Begin a PHP script with a statement to initialize two variables with the same integer value

```php
<?php
$a = $b = 5 ;
```

arguments.php

2. Next, define a function that accepts two integer arguments – one by value and the other by reference

```php
function modify( int $val , int &$ref )
{
    // Statements to be inserted here.
}
```

3. Now, insert statements to output the passed values, then increment those values and display the modified values

```php
echo "Passed values : $val , $ref<br>" ;
$val++ ;
$ref++ ;
echo "Incremented values : $val , $ref<hr>" ;
```

Don't forget

The **int** type description in this example specifies that only integer data values can be passed as arguments to the function.

4. After the function block add a statement to call the function, passing the variable values as arguments

```php
modify( $a , $b ) ;
```

5. Finally, add a statement to display the values now stored in each variable

```php
echo "Stored values : $a , $b" ;
?>
```

6. Save the document in your web server's **/htdocs** directory as **arguments.php** then open the page via HTTP to see the argument and variable values

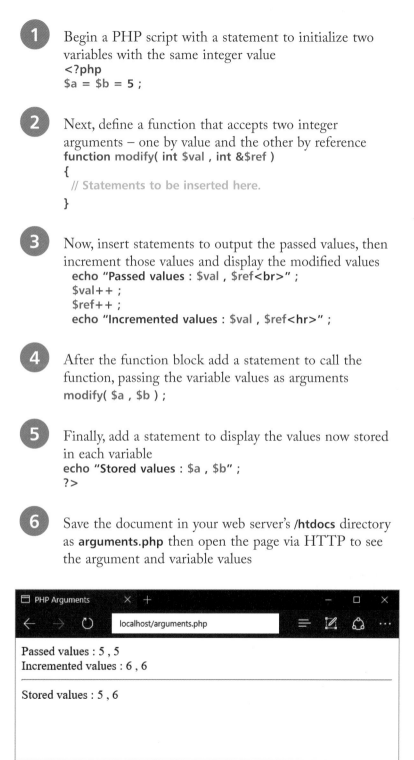

```
PHP Arguments        ×  +                    —  □  ×

←  →  ○    localhost/arguments.php       ≡  🖉  ◌  ...

Passed values : 5 , 5
Incremented values : 6 , 6
_____

Stored values : 5 , 6
```

Varying parameters

Default argument values can optionally be specified in a function definition by assignment to the parameter name, like this:

```
function function_name ( $arg_1 , $arg_2 = "Default String" )
{
  statement-to-be-executed ;
  statement-to-be-executed ;
  statement-to-be-executed ;
}
```

This allows a function call to be made that specifies either one or two argument values. If only one argument is specified, it is assigned to the first parameter and the default value is used by the second parameter. Where default values are specified for parameters, they must only appear in the parameter list following (to the right of) parameters that have no specified default value. Otherwise, a call without the correct total number of arguments would cause an error.

If you need to create a function that will accept an unknown number of arguments, PHP has a special ... "splat" operator for that purpose. This can be used in a function definition like this:

```
function function_name ( ...$args )
{
  statement-to-be-executed ;
  statement-to-be-executed ;
  statement-to-be-executed ;
}
```

When the ... splat operator is used to prefix a parameter name in a function definition, multiple arguments can be passed to that parameter to create an array. The array can be traversed like any other array to manipulate the passed in argument values.

Additionally, the ... splat operator can be used to "unpack" an array specified in a function call to pass its element values as individual arguments like this:

```
function function_name ( $arg_1 , $arg_2 , $arg_3 )
{
  echo $arg_1 + $arg_2 + $arg_3 ;
}

$arr = [ 1 , 2 , 3 ] ;

function_name ( ...$arr ) ;          # Outputs 6
```

Beware

If multiple default values are specified there is currently no way to skip a parameter in a function call, to assign an argument value to a particular parameter.

Hot tip

The ... splat operator is also sometimes known as the "scatter" operator.

1 Begin a PHP script by defining a function that provides default string values to its two parameters

```php
<?php
function drink( string $tmp = 'hot' , string $flavor = 'tea' )
{
  // Statement to be inserted here.
}
```

parameters.php

2 Next, insert a statement to display its default values or passed in argument values

```php
  echo "Drinking $tmp $flavor.<br>" ;
```

3 After the function block, add function calls that optionally pass string arguments

```php
drink() ; drink( 'iced' ) ; drink( 'cold' , 'lemonade' ) ;
```

4 Now, define a function that can accept multiple integer arguments and display their total value

```php
function add( int ...$numbers )
{
  $total = 0 ;
  foreach( $numbers as $num ) { $total += $num ; }
  echo "<hr>Total : $total" ;
}
```

5 Finally, after the function block add a statement to call the function in the previous step and pass three values

```php
add( 1 , 2 , 3 ) ;
?>
```

6 Save the document in your web server's **/htdocs** directory as **parameters.php** then open the page via HTTP to see the argument and default values

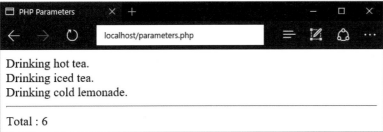

Hot tip

You can specify regular positional parameters before a parameter that accepts multiple arguments with the ... splat operator. Only arguments that outnumber the positional elements will be added to the array of the final parameter.

73

Recognizing scope

When creating custom functions it is important to understand how variable accessibility is limited by the variable's "scope":

- Variables created outside a function have "global" scope, but are not normally accessible from within any function block

- Variables created inside a function have "local" scope so are only accessible from within that particular function block

As a variable created within a function is not accessible from elsewhere, its name may duplicate the name of a variable outside a function block, or within another function block, without conflict. This allows a global variable to contain a different value to a local variable of the same name.

If you wish to use a global variable inside a function, you must first include a statement with the **global** keyword to declare that the variable name refers to a global variable, like this:

global *variable-name* **;**

The scope of a variable created within a function can be altered to make it available globally by preceding its declaration with the **global** keyword – but this is bad practice and should be avoided.

Function statements can call other functions to execute their statements and can also call themselves to execute recursively. As with loops, a recursive function must alter the state of a tested condition so it will not continue forever. This might be a counter value that gets passed in as an argument from an initial function call, then gets incremented on successive recursive calls until it exceeds a value specified in a test. Alternatively, a static local variable could be declared to store an incrementing value like this:

static *variable-name* **;**

Unlike other local variables, which lose their value when the program scope leaves the function, static variables retain their value. This means that the updated value of an incremented value stored in a static local variable is recognized on each function call.

A recursive function might otherwise reference a global variable counter value that gets incremented on successive recursive calls, until it exceeds a value specified in a test.

Beware

Global variables in PHP are not like those in other programming languages such as C, where they are automatically available to functions. In PHP, global variables can only be used in functions if first explicitly declared inside the function block using the **global** keyword.

74

1 Begin a PHP script by initializing a global variable with an integer and displaying the variable value

```php
<?php
$number = 1 ; echo "Global number : $number<br>" ;
```

scope.php

2 Next, define and call a function that initializes a like-named local variable and displays that variable value

```php
function show_local()
{
  $number = 100 ; echo "Local number : $number<hr>" ;
}
show_local() ;
```

3 Now, define and call a recursive function that increments the global variable and a static variable on each call

```php
function recur()
{
  global $number ;        static $letter = 'A' ;
  if( $number < 14 )
  {
    echo "$number:$letter | " ;
    $number++ ; $letter++ ; recur() ;
  }
}
recur() ;
```

If you remove the **static** keyword from this function the **$letter** variable will simply contain 'A' each time the function is called.

75

4 Finally, after the function block add a statement to display the modified global variable value

```php
echo "<hr>Global number : $number" ;
?>
```

5 Save the document in your web server's **/htdocs** directory as **scope.php** then open the page via HTTP to see the global and local variable values

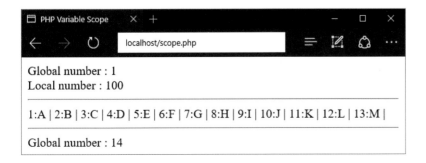

PHP also has a special **$GLOBALS** array in which the value of a global variable can be referenced by its name. In this example you could alternatively use **$GLOBALS['number']** to get the value.

Returning values

A custom PHP function can return a value to the caller by adding a statement using the **return** keyword, like this:

```
function function_name ( )
{
  statement-to-be-executed ;
  statement-to-be-executed ;
  return value ;
}
```

The **return** statement is optional and if omitted, functions will return a **NULL** value to the caller by default.

Functions can only return a single item to the caller, so they cannot return multiple values. You can, however, assign multiple values to elements of an array and have a function return the single array to the caller, then unpack the values.

A **return** statement can include an expression to be evaluated so its single result will be returned to the caller. For example:

```
function square( int $number )
{
  return $number * $number ;
}

echo square( 3 ) ;          # Outputs 9
```

To ensure a function will only return a value of a desired data type, the function declaration can, optionally, specify the return type description such as **int**, **float**, **string**, **bool** or **array**, like this:

```
function function_name ( ) : int
{
  statement-to-be-executed ;
  statement-to-be-executed ;
  return value ;
}
```

When a return data type is specified, a function that attempts to return an incorrect data type to the caller will result in an error.

The ability to specify a return data type is a new feature in PHP 7.

1. Begin a PHP script by defining a function that must only return an array of data

```php
<?php
function supply() : array
{
  // Statement to be inserted here.
}
```

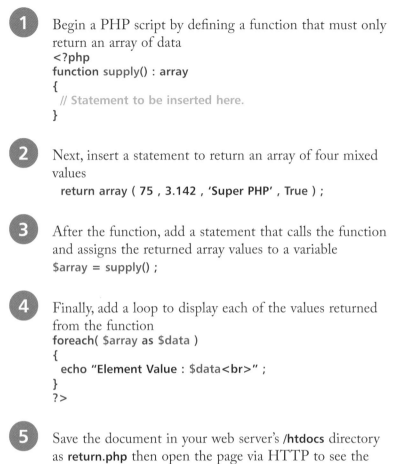

return.php

2. Next, insert a statement to return an array of four mixed values

```php
return array ( 75 , 3.142 , 'Super PHP' , True ) ;
```

3. After the function, add a statement that calls the function and assigns the returned array values to a variable

```php
$array = supply() ;
```

4. Finally, add a loop to display each of the values returned from the function

```php
foreach( $array as $data )
{
  echo "Element Value : $data<br>" ;
}
?>
```

5. Save the document in your web server's **/htdocs** directory as **return.php** then open the page via HTTP to see the returned values

```
Element Value : 75
Element Value : 3.142
Element Value : Super PHP
Element Value : 1
```

In PHP the Boolean **TRUE** value is represented numerically as 1.

Calling back

PHP allows you to create "anonymous" functions that have no name specified in the function definition. Like other functions, these can accept arguments if parameters are specified and they can optionally return a value when called. Unlike other function definitions, which are code constructs, an anonymous function definition is an expression. This means that each anonymous function definition must be terminated by a semicolon, like this:

```
function ( )
{
  statement-to-be-executed ;
  statement-to-be-executed ;
  return value ;
} ;
```

On its own an anonymous function is of little use as, without a name, it cannot be called, but it can be useful in other ways:

- Assigned to a variable, an anonymous function can be called using the variable name

- Passed as a callable argument to another function, an anonymous function can be called later as a "callback"

- Returned from a function, an anonymous function retains access to the returning function's variables in "closure"

By assigning an anonymous function to a variable you do, in effect, give the function a name and can call it and pass it arguments as you would any other function – using the variable name. Similarly, when you pass an anonymous function to another function it can be called back and passed arguments as you would any other function – using the parameter name. The PHP **use** keyword and **&** ampersand prefix allows an anonymous function to reference a local variable in the returning function.

Beware

Don't forget to add a terminating **;** semicolon after each anonymous function definition.

callback.php

1. Begin a PHP script by assigning to a variable an anonymous function that accepts a single argument
```
<?php
$hello = function ( $user ) { echo "Hello $user!<br>" ; } ;
```

2. Next, add a statement that calls the anonymous function and passes a single argument
```
$hello( 'Mike' ) ;
```

3 Now, define a regular function that accepts a single callable argument and calls that function passing a string

```php
function greet( callable $anon )
{
  $anon( 'Carole Anne' ) ;
}
```

4 Add a statement to call the function, defined in the previous step, passing the anonymous function that was assigned to a variable in the first step

```php
greet( $hello ) ;
```

5 Next, define another regular function, which has one local variable and returns an anonymous function that references the local variable value

```php
function meet() : callable
{
  $time = 'morning' ;
  return function( $name ) use( &$time )
  { return "Good $time, $name!" ; } ;
}
```

Don't forget

Remember to include the & ampersand prefix to create a reference to the variable value.

6 Assign to a variable the function defined in the previous step then call that function, passing a string argument

```php
$meeting = meet() ;
echo $meeting( 'Susan' ) ;
?>
```

7 Save the document in your web server's **/htdocs** directory as **callback.php** then open the page via HTTP to see the returned values from anonymous functions

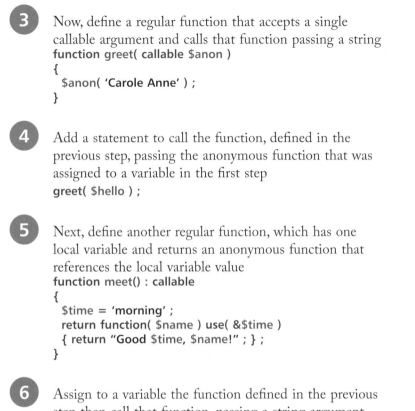

PHP Callback

localhost/callback.php

Hello Mike!
Hello Carole Anne!
Good morning, Susan!

Hot tip

Notice that the final function call gets the 'morning' string from the parent scope.

Summary

- Custom functions allow PHP scripts to be modularized into sections of code that are easier to understand and maintain

- Function names must begin with a letter or underscore character and are not case-sensitive

- A function is defined by stating its name after the **function** keyword, then parentheses and braces containing statements

- A function accepting arguments is defined by including a comma-separated list of parameters within the parentheses

- Optionally, a function definition can specify the type of data to be passed from the caller by including a data type description before the parameter name

- Argument data is normally passed by value but can be passed by reference if the parameter name is given an **&** prefix

- Default argument values can optionally be specified in a function definition by assignment to the parameter name

- When a parameter name is given a ... splat operator prefix, multiple arguments can be passed to that parameter to create an array

- Variables created outside a function have global scope, but are not accessible from within a function block unless it includes a declaration using the **global** keyword

- Variables created inside a function have local scope so are only accessible from within that particular function block

- Local variables lose their value when the program scope leaves the function, but **static** variables retain their value

- The **return** keyword returns a single item to the caller and the function definition can optionally specify the return data type

- An anonymous function definition does not specify a name but is an expression so must end with a ; semicolon

- The **use** keyword and **&** ampersand prefix allow an anonymous function to reference a local variable in the returning function

6 Manipulating strings

This chapter demonstrates various ways to manipulate text strings in PHP scripts.

Comparing characters

PHP provides a number of built-in functions to perform a comparison of two text strings. The simple **strcmp()** function accepts two string arguments for comparison and will return one of three integer values depending on the result. When the strings exactly match, **strcmp()** will return zero. When the first string argument is greater than the second, **strcmp()** will return 1, but when the first string argument is less than the second, **strcmp()** will return -1.

The **strncmp()** function works in a similar way, but accepts a third integer argument to specify the number of characters from the start of the strings to be compared.

The **strcmp()** and **strncmp()** functions attach different importance to uppercase and lowercase characters when comparing strings. When you prefer to ignore case, you can use the alternative companion functions **strcasecmp()** and **strncasecmp()** instead.

To appreciate the results from each of the four comparison functions it is useful to understand how the comparisons are actually made. Each character has a standard numerical "ASCII" value where lowercase a-z is in the range 97-122 and uppercase A-Z is in the range 65-90. Comparing the first value in each range we see that "a" (97) is greater than "A" (65). Supplying these as arguments the **strcmp()** function would therefore return 1, as the first argument is greater than the second. Conversely, if you specify "A" (65) as the first argument and "a" (97) as the second argument then the **strcmp()** function would return -1, as the first argument is less than the second. With string comparisons, each character is compared in sequence to ensure that strings containing the same characters in different order are not seen to be incorrectly equal. For example, comparing "ABC" and "BAC" the first character "A" (65) is less than first character "B" (66) so the **strcmp()** function would return -1, as the first argument is less than the second.

The ASCII value of any character can be found by specifying the character as an argument to the PHP **ord()** function, and the length of a string can be found by specifying it as the argument to the PHP **strlen()** function.

Beware

Strictly speaking, the **strcmp()** returned values will be a positive integer, zero, or a negative integer – but are typically values of 1, 0, or -1.

Hot tip

ASCII is an abbreviation for the American Standard Code for Information Exchange that specifies the universal standard character coding scheme.

1 Begin a PHP script with statements to initialize four
variables with string values
```php
<?php
$str1 = 'PHP In Easy Steps' ;
$str2 = 'PHP In Easy Steps' ;
$str3 = 'PHP Easy Steps' ;
$str4 = 'php in easy steps' ;
```

characters.php

2 Next, add statements to compare the strings
```php
echo "'$str1' versus '$str2' : ".strcmp($str1, $str2).'<br>' ;
echo "'$str1' versus '$str3' : ".strcmp($str1, $str3).'<br>' ;
echo "'$str1' versus '$str4' : ".strcmp($str1, $str4).'<hr>' ;
```

3 Now, add a statement for a case-insensitive comparison
```php
echo 'Comparison Ignoring Case :<br>' ;
echo "'$str1' versus '$str4' : ".strcasecmp($str1, $str4) ;
```

4 Finally, add a loop to count and display the total ASCII
code value of the first string
```php
$total = 0 ;
for ( $i = 0 ; $i < strlen( $str1 ) ; $i++ )
{
  $total += ord( $str1[ $i ] ) ;
}
echo "<hr>ASCII Total $str1 : $total" ;
?>
```

5 Save the document in your web server's **/htdocs** directory
as **characters.php** then open the page via HTTP to see
the string comparisons

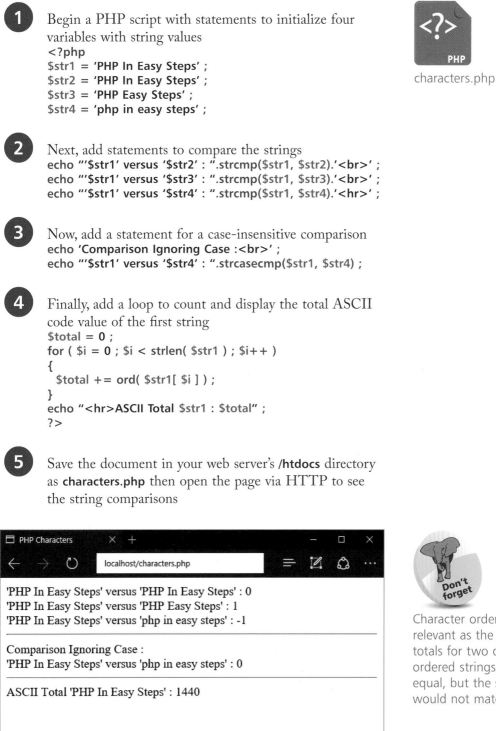

83

Character order is
relevant as the ASCII
totals for two differently
ordered strings could be
equal, but the strings
would not match.

Searching text

PHP provides a number of built-in functions to search a string to find a specified substring or single character. The simple **strpos()** function accepts two arguments to specify the string in which to search, and the substring to find. It will search in sequence from the start of the string to find a match. When a match is found the search halts and the **strpos()** function returns an integer, which is the character index number position within the string at which the first occurrence of a match begins. When no match is found the **strpos()** function returns **FALSE**.

The **strrpos()** function works in a similar way but returns the index number position at which the first occurrence of a match begins when searching in reverse order, from the end of the string.

Other PHP search functions can return a part of the searched string, rather than an index number indicating a match position.

The **strstr()** function accepts two arguments to specify the string in which to search, and the substring to find. It will search in sequence from the start of the string to find a match. When a match is found, the search halts and the **strstr()** function returns the remainder of the searched string from where the first occurrence of a match begins. When no match is found the **strstr()** function returns **NULL**.

Similarly, where character case is unimportant, you can use the companion **stristr()** function to make a case-insensitive search. This will return the remainder of the searched string from where the first occurrence of a case-insensitive match begins.

The **strchr()** function works in a similar way but accepts two arguments to specify the string in which to search, and a single character to find. As you might expect, the companion **strrchr()** function begins searching in reverse order, from the end of the string. Both return the remainder of the searched string from where the first occurrence of a match begins.

Beware

Notice that there is no **strrstr()** (companion function to **strstr()**) to search in reverse order.

1 Begin a PHP script with statements to initialize a variable with a string value and report its length

```php
<?php
$str = 'Most Users usually find PHP useful.' ;
echo "'$str'<br>String Length : ".strlen( $str ) ;
```

search.php

2 Next, add statements to search the string, both forwards and reverse, and report the position of a given substring

```php
echo "<br>First 'us' found at : ".strpos( $str , 'us' ) ;
echo "<br>Final 'us' found at : ".strrpos( $str , 'us' ) ;
```

3 Now, add statements to search the string, both case-sensitive and case-insensitive, and return the remainder of the string following a substring match

```php
echo "<hr>Substring from first 'us' : ".strstr( $str , 'us' ) ;
echo "<br>Substring from first 'us' case insensitive : "
                              .stristr( $str , 'us' ) ;
```

4 Finally, add statements to search the string, both forwards and reverse, and return the remainder of the string following a character match

```php
echo "<hr>Characters from first 'u' : ".strchr( $str , 'u' ) ;
echo "<br>Characters from final 'u' : ".strrchr( $str , 'u' ) ;
?>
```

5 Save the document in your web server's **/htdocs** directory as **search.php** then open the page via HTTP to see the search results

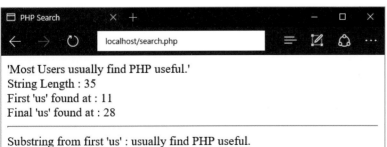

There are three occurrences of 'us' in this string, but only the first and third are matched.

Extracting substrings

A substring can be extracted from a string by stating the string, and index position of a substring within the string, as arguments to the **substr()** function. Optionally, a third argument can specify the substring length. You may replace a substring using the **substr_replace()** function to specify string, substring, index position and length arguments. The total number of occurrences of a substring within a string can be found using the **substr_count()** function:

substring.php

 Begin a PHP script with statements to initialize a variable with a string value and count substrings
```php
<?php
$str = 'SQL in easy steps features SQL queries' ;
echo "'$str'<br>'SQL' Count: ".substr_count( $str , 'SQL' ) ;
```

 Next, add statements to extract two substrings
```php
echo '<hr>Index 27 : '.substr( $str , 27 ) ;
echo '<hr>Index 4 Length 13 : '.substr( $str , 4 , 13 ) ;
```

 Now, add a statement to initialize a variable with a string
```php
$sub = 'PHP & MySQL' ;
```

 Finally, add statements to replace a substring with a new string value and to display the modified string
```php
$str = substr_replace( $str, $sub , 0 , 3 ) ;
echo "<hr>'$str'" ;
?>
```

5 Save the document in your web browser's **/htdocs** directory as **substring.php** then open the page via HTTP to see the extracted substrings and modified string

The length argument in **substr_replace()** specifies the length of the substring to be replaced. In this example, it is **3** – to replace the three characters 'SQL' with a longer string.

Changing case

PHP provides functions to easily modify the character case of a specified string argument. The **strtolower()** function changes all characters to lowercase and **strtoupper()** changes them all to uppercase. Additionally, the **ucfirst()** function makes only the first string character uppercase, whereas the **ucword()** function makes the first character of every word in the string into uppercase:

1 Begin a PHP script with statements to initialize a variable with a string and display its value
```
<?php
$str = "C++ Programming in easy steps" ;
echo "Original String : '$str' <hr>" ;
```

case.php

2 Next, add statements to display a lowercase version
```
$ver = strtolower( $str ) ;
echo "Lowercase String : '$ver' <br>" ;
```

3 Now, add statements to display an uppercase version
```
$ver = strtoupper( $str ) ;
echo "Uppercase String : '$ver' <hr>" ;
```

4 Finally, add statements to display a capitalized string version and a capitalized words version
```
$ver = ucfirst( strtolower( $str ) ) ;
echo "Uppercase First String Character : '$ver' <br>" ;
echo 'Uppercase First Word Character : '.ucwords( $ver ) ;
?>
```

The **ucfirst()** function only changes the first character of a string. Other uppercase characters will remain unless first changed to lowercase with the **strtolower()** function, as seen here.

5 Save the document in your web server's **/htdocs** directory as **case.php** then open the page via HTTP to see the changed case versions of the original string

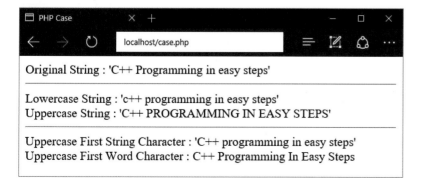

Formatting strings

PHP provides a number of built-in functions to conveniently format strings by manipulating their characters. The simple **strrev()** function accepts a single string argument and returns that string in reversed character order, so it reads back to front.

The **strrpt()** function accepts two arguments to specify a string, and an integer of how many total times that string should be repeated in the string it will return.

The **strpad()** function accepts three arguments to specify a string, a total length of the character string it will return, and a character or substring pattern with which to fill the difference between the original string and the specified returned string length. The padding will, by default, be added to the end of the original string but can be added to its start by adding a fourth argument using a special **STR_PAD_LEFT** flag.

The **trim()** function can accept a single string argument and will return a string in which all white-space characters (spaces, line returns, tabs) have been removed from the start and end of the original string. Optionally, a second argument can specify a character or pattern to be removed from the start and end of the original string, in place of the white-space default.

Similarly, where you only want to remove characters from the start of the original string, you can use the companion **ltrim()** function, or where you only want to remove characters from the end of the original string, you can use the companion **rtrim()** function.

A string can be split into individual parts using the **strtok()** function to specify the string and a delimiter token around which the parts should be split. For example, if you want to split a string into individual words you can specify the space character as the delimiter token. The first part of the string, up to the delimiter token will be returned by the function. Interestingly, the **strtok()** function remembers its position in the string, so subsequent calls need only specify the delimiter token to return the next part of the string, until no further delimiters are found. Splitting a string in this way can best be achieved using a loop to make subsequent calls to the **strtok()** function, until it reaches the end of the string.

Hot tip

The PHP **implode()** and **explode()** functions can be used to convert arrays to strings, and strings to arrays – see page 28 for more details.

1 Begin a PHP script with statements to initialize a variable with a string and display its value

```php
<?php
$str = '| PHP String Fun |' ; echo "Original String : $str" ;
```

format.php

2 Next, add statements to display reversed, repeated and trimmed versions of the original string

```php
echo '<hr>Reversed String : '.strrev( $str ) ;
echo '<hr>Repeated String : '.str_repeat( $str , 3 ) ;
echo '<hr>Trimmed String : '.trim( $str, '|' ) ;
```

3 Now, add a statements to display a 30-character version of the string, padded with asterisks at the beginning

```php
$pad = str_pad( $str , 30 , '*' , STR_PAD_LEFT ) ;
echo "<hr>Padded String : $pad" ;
```

4 Finally, add statements to split the string around spaces and display each individual part separated by an ... ellipsis

```php
echo '<hr>Split String : ' ;
$token = strtok( $str , ' ' );
while ( $token )
{
  echo "$token ... " ; $token = strtok( ' ' ) ;
}
?>
```

> **Don't forget**
>
> You must specify the delimiter on each subsequent call to **strtok()** to have it continue forward to the next part of the string.

5 Save the document in your web server's **/htdocs** directory as **format.php** then open the page via HTTP to see the string formatted in several ways

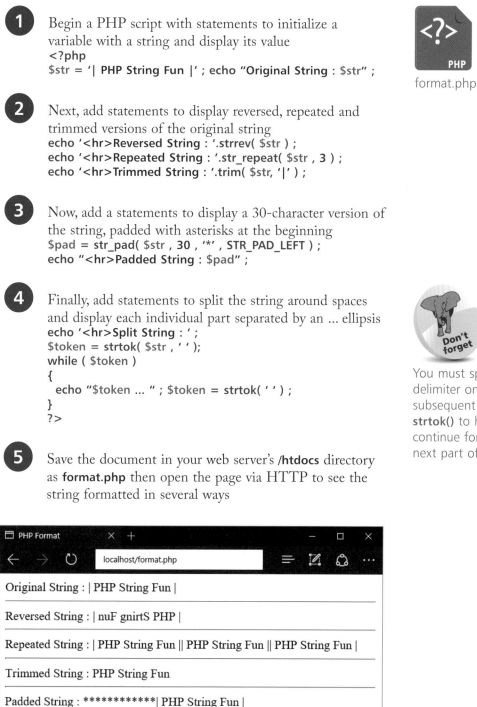

Original String : | PHP String Fun |

Reversed String : | nuF gnirtS PHP |

Repeated String : | PHP String Fun || PHP String Fun || PHP String Fun |

Trimmed String : PHP String Fun

Padded String : ************| PHP String Fun |

Split String : | ... PHP ... String ... Fun ... | ...

Making dates

The PHP **date()** function will return a date string when called, but requires a string argument to specify a format for the date string. This format string can comprise a series of letter options for date and time. For example, **date('n/j/y')** might return "4/22/16". Popular options are listed below along with a brief description:

Option:	Description:	Example:
Y	Year as four digits	2014
y	Year as two digits	14
n	Month as one or two digits	7
m	Month as two digits	07
F	Month full name	February
M	Month name as three letters	Feb
j	Day as one or two digits	4
d	Day as two digits	04
l	Weekday full name	Monday
D	Weekday as three letters	Mon
S	Ordinal suffix as two letters	th
H	Hour in 24-hour format	14
i	Minutes	45
s	Seconds	30
a	Ante or post meridiem	am

Beware

The weekday full name option is a lowercase "L".

Hot tip

You can discover more **date()** function options in the PHP manual online at **php.net/manual**

By default, the timezone is set to the Universal Time Clock (UTC) but you can set it to your own timezone by specifying it as an argument to the **date_default_timezone_set()** function, and see the currently set timezone with **date_default_timezone_get()**.

You may also create your own timestamp using the intelligent **strtotime()** function. This can accept a date string argument and return a timestamp that can be supplied as an optional second argument to the **date()** function. The argument specified to **strtotime()** can be a regular text date, such as "July 4, 2017". Additionally, you can specify an argument such as "yesterday", "+3months" or "next Wednesday" and the **strtotime()** function will try to figure it out and return an appropriate timestamp.

...cont'd

1 Begin a PHP script with statements to display the current date, day, time and current default timezone

```php
<?php
echo 'Date : '.date( 'jS F Y' ).'<br>' ;
echo 'Day : '.date( 'l' ).'<br>' ;
echo 'Time : '.date( 'h:i:s a' ).'<br>' ;
echo 'Timezone : '.date_default_timezone_get().'<hr>' ;
```

date.php

2 Next, add statements to change the default timezone and display a confirmation, then show the current time there

```php
date_default_timezone_set( 'America/New_York' ) ;
echo 'Timezone now : '.date_default_timezone_get() ;
echo '<br>Time now : '.date( 'h:i:s a' ).'<hr>' ;
```

Notice that you can include separator characters such as : and / in the format string.

3 Now, add statements to create a timestamp for the next day, then display its day name and date

```php
$d = strtotime( 'tomorrow' ) ;
echo 'Tomorrow : '.date( 'l, jS F Y' , $d ).'<br>' ;
```

4 Finally, add statements to create a timestamp for a memorable date, then display its month and day number

```php
$d = strtotime( 'July 11, 1994' ) ;
echo 'David\'s Birthday : '.date( 'F jS' , $d ) ;
?>
```

5 Save the document in your web server's **/htdocs** directory as **date.php** then open the page via HTTP to see the date strings formatted by the options

```
┌─────────────────────────────────────────────────────────┐
│ 🗖 PHP Date        ×  +              —   □   ×          │
│ ←  →  ↻    localhost/date.php        ≡  🖊  ⌂  ...      │
├─────────────────────────────────────────────────────────┤
│ Date : 22nd April 2016                                  │
│ Day : Friday                                            │
│ Time : 10:05:16 am                                      │
│ Timezone : UTC                                          │
│ ─────────────────────────────────────────────────      │
│ Timezone now : America/New_York                         │
│ Time now : 06:05:16 am                                  │
│ ─────────────────────────────────────────────────      │
│ Tomorrow : Saturday, 23rd April 2016                    │
│ David's Birthday : July 11th                            │
└─────────────────────────────────────────────────────────┘
```

Some countries prefer date order of M/D/Y while others prefer D/M/Y so you can choose your preferred date format options.

Encoding entities

There are two PHP functions available to encode HTML code, so that all characters of special significance or unusual characters are replaced by "entity" equivalents. The **htmlentities()** function encodes all characters below, which each have an entity equivalent:

```
" & < >   ¡ ¢ £ ¤ ¥ ¦ § ¨ © ª « ¬ ® ¯ ° ± ² ³ ´ µ ¶ · ¸ ¹ º » ¼ ½ ¾ ¿ À Á Â Ã Ä
Å Æ Ç È É Ê Ë Ì Í Î Ï Ð Ñ Ò Ó Ô Õ Ö × Ø Ù Ú Û Ü Ý Þ ß à á â ã ä å æ ç è
é ê ë ì í î ï ð ñ ò ó ô õ ö ÷ ø ù ú û ü ý þ ÿ Œ œ Š š Ÿ ƒ ˆ ˜ Α Β Γ Δ Ε Ζ Η Θ Ι
Κ Λ Μ Ν Ξ Ο Π Ρ Σ Τ Υ Φ Χ Ψ Ω α β γ δ ε ζ η θ ι κ λ μ ν ξ ο π ρ ς σ τ υ φ
χ ψ ω ϑ ϒ ϖ        – — ' ' „ " " … † ‡ • … ‰ ' ″ ‹ › ‾ ⁄ € ℑ ℘ ℜ ™ ℵ ← ↑
→ ↓ ↔ ↵ ⇐ ⇑ ⇒ ⇓ ⇔ ∀ ∂ ∃ ∅ ∇ ∈ ∉ ∋ ∏ ∑ − ∗ √ ∝ ∞ ∠ ∧ ∨ ∩ ∪ ∫ ∴ ~ ≅
≈ ≠ ≡ ≤ ≥ ⊂ ⊃ ⊄ ⊆ ⊇ ⊕ ⊗ ⊥ ⋅ ⌈ ⌉ ⌊ ⌋ ⟨ ⟩ ◊ ♠ ♣ ♥ ♦
```

Unless you are concerned about non-English language characters, it is generally preferable to use the alternative **htmlspecialchars()** function to encode only characters of special HTML significance:

- & ampersand – becomes **&**

- " double quote – becomes **"**

- ' single quote – becomes **'**

- < less than – becomes **<**

- > greater than – becomes **>**

One good reason to encode HTML snippets with PHP is to prevent malicious JavaScript code being executed unintentionally by the web browser. Encoding HTML tags into entities ensures that the HTML **<script>** tag will not be recognized, so its JavaScript code contents will not be executed:

encode.php

1 Create a PHP script with statements to initialize a variable with an HTML snippet and display its value
```php
<?php
$html = '<script>window.location="index.html"</script>' ;
// Statement to be inserted here.
echo $html ;
?>
```

2 Save the document in your web server's **/htdocs** directory as **encode.php** then open the page via HTTP to hopefully see the HTML code snippet

...cont'd

The browser has interpreted the code and relocated to the server's index page because it recognized the HTML **<script>** tag.

 3 Return to the PHP script and insert a statement to encode special HTML characters
$html = htmlspecialchars($html) ;

4 Save the edited document and reopen the page via HTTP again to see the HTML code snippet

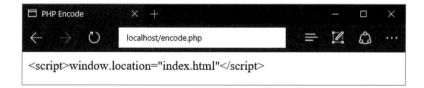

5 Use the **View Source** facility in your web browser to see the special character entity equivalents encoded by PHP

```
/encode.php - F12 Developer Tools - Microsoft Edge           —   □   ×
F12   DOM Explorer    Console    Debugger    Network ▶ ▼        ▷ | ? ⊞ ▭
▶  ‖  ↳. ↳. ↳. ⇥ ⬤▾ ↗ 🔒 📄              Find (Ctrl+F)
📁▾   encode.php   ✕                         ⬚ 💾 ⇥ ⇄ ⬚ 🐞
  1 <!DOCTYPE HTML>
  2 <html lang="en">
  3 <head>
  4 <meta charset="UTF-8">
  5 <title>PHP Encode</title>
  6 </head>
  7 <body>
  8 &lt;script&gt;window.location=&quot;index.html&quot;&lt;/script&gt;</body>
  9 </html>
```

Hot tip

The PHP function **html_entity_decode()** can be used to unencode all entities back to their original character state.

Summary

- The PHP built-in string comparison functions **strcmp()**, **strncmp()**, **strcasecmp()** and **strncasecmp()** each typically return a result of 1 (greater), 0 (equal) or -1 (less)

- String comparisons are based on the numerical ASCII value of each character, compared in sequence to account for order

- The ASCII value of any character can be found using **ord()**

- The length of any string can be found using **strlen()**

- The numerical index position of a substring within a searched string can be found using **strpos()** and **strrpos()** functions

- The search functions **strstr()**, **stristr()**, **strchr()** and **strrchr()** each return the remainder of a searched string on success

- The substring functions **substr()**, **substr_replace()** and **substr_count()** can extract, replace or count occurrences

- The characters in a string can be reversed using **strrev()**, or the string can be repeated using **strrpt()**

- Padding characters can be added to a string using **strpad()** and characters can be removed using **trim()**, **ltrim()** or **rtrim()**

- A string can be split into individual parts by specifying a delimiter to the **strtok()** function

- The **date()** function requires a string argument that specifies options to determine the format of its returned date string

- By default the PHP date timezone is set to UTC

- The **date_default_timezone_set()** function can be used to specify an alternative to the UTC default timezone

- The **strtotime()** function will attempt to return an appropriate timestamp for whatever date or time argument it receives

- The **htmlentities()** function will encode all string characters for which there is an equivalent entity

- The **htmlspecialchars()** function will encode only characters of special HTML significance to avoid recognition by a browser

7 Building classes

Encapsulating data

A class is a data structure that can contain both variables and functions in a single entity. These are collectively known as its "members" – the variables are known as its class "properties" and the functions are known as its class "methods".

Access to class members from outside the class is controlled by "access specifiers" in the class declaration. Typically, these will deny access to the class variables but allow access to methods that can store and retrieve data from those variable members. This technique of "data hiding" ensures that stored data is safely encapsulated within the class variable members, and is the first principle of Object Oriented Programming (OOP).

A class declaration begins with the **class** keyword, followed by a space, then a programmer-specified name – adhering to the usual PHP naming conventions but beginning in uppercase. Next come the class property declarations followed by the class method declarations. These are like regular variable and function declarations but should each begin with an access specifier. The class declaration syntax looks like this:

```
class ClassName
{
  access-specifier $var1 , $var2 , $var3 ;

  access-specifier functionName1 ( $arg1 , $arg2 , $arg3 )
  {
    statements-to-execute ;
  }
}
```

An access specifier may be any one of the keywords **public, private** or **protected**, to specify access rights for its listed members:

- **public** members are accessible from any place where the class is visible

- **private** members are accessible only to other members of the same class in which they are defined

- **protected** members are accessible only to other members of the same class and members of classes derived from that class

It is conventional to begin class names with an uppercase character and object names with lowercase.

Derived classes are introduced later in this chapter – see page 104.

Any real-world object can be defined by its attributes and by its actions. For example, a dog has attributes such as age, weight and color, and actions it can perform such as bark. The class mechanism in PHP provides a way to create a virtual dog object within a script, where the class properties can represent its attributes and the class methods represent its actions:

```php
class Dog
{
  private $age ;
  private $weight ;
  private $color ;

  public function bark() { echo 'WOOF!' ; }

  // Plus methods here to store data in the properties.

  // Plus methods here to retrieve data from the properties.

}
```

off

The Don't forget icon text:

While a PHP script class cannot perfectly emulate a real-word object, the aim is to encapsulate all relevant attributes and actions as class properties and methods.

It is important to recognize that a class declaration only defines a data structure – in order to create an object you must declare an "instance" of that data structure. This is achieved by assigning a copy of a class to a variable using the **new** keyword, like this:

```php
$fido = new Dog() ;    // Creates an instance named "fido"
                       // of the programmer-defined
                       // "Dog" data structure.
```

The instance object is a working copy of the original class data structure so retains all its features. As the method in the example above has been declared **public**, it is visible in the script outside the class declaration. This means the instance's copy of the method can be called using a special -> object operator, like this:

```php
$fido->bark() ;        // Outputs WOOF!
```

Notice that you must add parentheses after the class name in the statement creating an instance object.

The -> object operator can be used to reference any visible class member, but the variable properties in the example above have been declared **private** so are encapsulated in the object and are not directly accessible. The principle of encapsulation in PHP programming describes the grouping together of data and functionality in class members – these are the age, weight, color attributes and bark action in this Dog class.

Creating an object

In order to assign and retrieve data from private members of a class, special **public** accessor methods must be added to the class. These are "setter" methods to assign data, and "getter" methods to retrieve data. Accessor methods are often named as the variable they address, with the first letter made uppercase, and prefixed by "set" or "get" respectively. For example, accessor methods to address an **age** variable may be named **setAge()** and **getAge()**.

The setter and getter methods can reference a member of the same class using a special **$this** "pseudo-variable", followed by the **->** object operator, and the property name. For example, using **$this->age** to reference an age property:

object.php

Hot tip

In the class declaration, notice that all methods are declared public and all variables are declared private. This notion of "public interface, private data" is a key concept when creating classes.

1 Begin a PHP script with a statement to declare a class named "Dog"
```php
<?php
class Dog
{
    // Members to be inserted here (steps 2-5).
}
```

2 Between the braces of the Dog class declaration, declare three private variable members
```php
private $age ;
private $weight ;
private $color ;
```

3 After the private variables, add a public method to output a string when called
```php
public function bark() { echo 'WOOF! WOOF! <br>' ; }
```

4 Add public setter methods – to assign individual argument values to each of the private variables
```php
public function setAge ( int $yrs )
{ $this->age = $yrs ; }

public function setWeight ( int $lbs )
{ $this->weight = $lbs ; }

public function setColor ( string $fur )
{ $this->color = $fur ; }
```

...cont'd

5 Add public getter methods – to retrieve individual values from each of the private variables

```
public function getAge() { return $this->age ; }

public function getWeight() { return $this->weight ; }

public function getColor() { return $this->color ; }
```

Fido

6 After the Dog class declaration, declare an instance of the Dog class named "fido"

```
$fido = new Dog() ;
```

7 Add statements calling each setter method to assign data

```
$fido->setAge( 3 ) ;
$fido->setWeight( 15 ) ;
$fido->setColor( 'brown' ) ;
```

8 Add statements calling each getter method to retrieve the assigned values

```
echo 'Fido is a '.$fido->getColor().' dog <br>' ;
echo 'Fido is '.$fido->getAge().' years old <br>' ;
echo 'Fido weighs '.$fido->getWeight().' pounds<br>' ;
```

A new feature in PHP 7 is the ability to also create "anonymous classes" with simple functionality and no name. For example,
```
$util = new class {
public function log($s) {
echo $s ; } } ;
```
that can be called with
```
$util->log( 'Data' ) ;
```

9 Now, add a call to the regular output method

```
$fido->bark() ;
?>
```

10 Save the document in your web server's **/htdocs** directory as **object.php** then open the page via HTTP to see the output class properties and method call

Hot tip

This **object.php** script will get modified over the next few pages as new features are incorporated.

Initializing members

A program can easily create multiple objects simply by declaring multiple instances of a class, and each object can have unique attributes by assigning individual values with its setter methods.

It is often convenient to combine the setter methods into a single method that accepts arguments for each private variable. This means that all values can be assigned with a single statement in the program, but the method will contain multiple statements.

Optionally, each parameter can specify a permissible data type for each argument being passed, and may also usefully specify default values to each parameter:

initializer.php

 Rename a copy of the previous example "object.php" as a new program "initializer.php"

 In the Dog class declaration, replace the three setter methods with a single combined setter method that specifics the argument data types and default values
```
public function setValues
( int $yrs = 2 , int $lbs = 8 , string $fur = 'black' )
{
    // Statements to be inserted here.
}
```

3 In the method definition block, insert three statements to assign values from passed arguments to class variables
```
$this->age = $yrs ;
$this->weight = $lbs ;
$this->color = $fur ;
```

4 After the modified class definition, replace the calls to the three setter methods by a single call to the combined setter method – passing three arguments
```
$fido->setValues( 3 , 15 , 'brown' ) ;
```

 Declare a second instance of the Dog class named "pooch"
```
$pooch = new Dog() ;
```

 Add a second call to the combined setter method – passing three arguments for the new object
```
$pooch->setValues( 4, 18, 'gray' ) ;
```

Hot tip

Try passing an incorrect data type to the initializer method to see a type error occur.

7 Add statements calling each getter method to retrieve the assigned values
```
echo '<hr>Pooch: '.$pooch->getAge().'yrs' ;
echo $pooch->getWeight().'lbs '.$pooch->getColor() ;
```

8 Add a second call to the regular output method
```
$pooch->bark() ;
```

9 Now, declare a third instance of the Dog class named "rover"
```
$rover = new Dog() ;
```

10 Add a third call to the combined setter method – this time passing no arguments for the new object
```
$rover->setValues( ) ;
```

11 Add statements calling each getter method to retrieve the assigned values, which are specified default values
```
echo '<hr>Rover: '.$rover->getAge().'yrs' ;
echo $rover->getWeight().'lbs '.$rover->getColor() ;
```

You must still call the initializer method here, to assign the default values to the class variables when passing no arguments.

12 Add a third call to the regular output method
```
$rover->bark() ;
```

13 Save the document in your web server's **/htdocs** directory as **initializer.php** then open the page via HTTP to see the output set by the combined initializer method

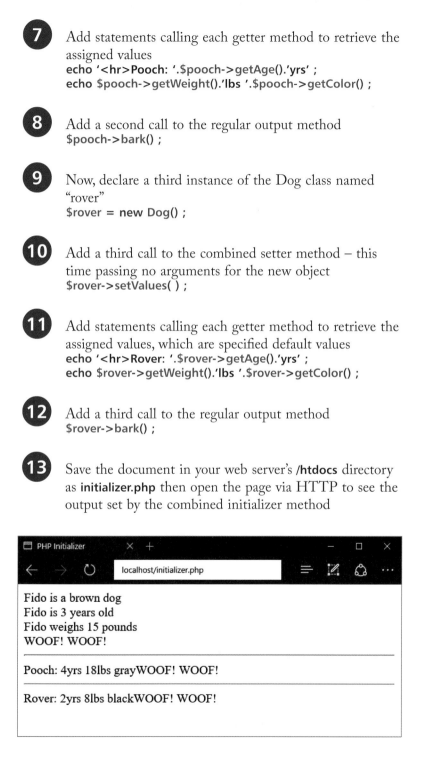

PHP Initializer — □ ✕

localhost/initializer.php

Fido is a brown dog
Fido is 3 years old
Fido weighs 15 pounds
WOOF! WOOF!

Pooch: 4yrs 18lbs grayWOOF! WOOF!

Rover: 2yrs 8lbs blackWOOF! WOOF!

Using constructors

Class variable members can be initialized by a special "constructor" method that is called whenever an instance of the class is created. The constructor method is always named **__construct()** and can accept arguments to set the initial value of class variables.

A constructor method has a companion "destructor" method – that is called whenever an instance of the class is destroyed. The destructor method is always named **__destruct()**.

Constructor and destructor methods have no return value and are called automatically – they cannot be called explicitly, and consequently their declarations need no access specifier.

Values to initialize class variables are passed to the constructor method in the statement creating an object, in parentheses following the object name:

constructor.php

 Rename a copy of the previous example "initializer.php" as a new program "constructor.php"

 In the Dog class declaration, replace the setValues method with this constructor
```
function __construct
( int $yrs = 2 , int $lbs = 8 , string $fur = 'black' )
{
  $this->age = $yrs ;
  $this->weight = $lbs ;
  $this->color = $fur ;
}
```

 Now, add a simple destructor method
```
function __destruct() { echo '<hr>Object Destroyed.' ; }
```

Hot tip

The definition of a class method is also known as the method "implementation".

4 After the Dog class declaration, edit the statement creating the "fido" object – to pass values to its constructor method, in order to initialize properties
```
$fido = new Dog( 3 , 15 , 'brown' ) ;
```

5 Similarly, edit the statement creating the "pooch" object – to pass values to the constructor method
```
$pooch = new Dog( 4 , 18 , 'gray' ) ;
```

6 Also edit the statement creating the "rover" object – to use default values of the constructor method
```
$rover = new Dog( ) ;
```

7 Delete the statements calling the setValues method of all three objects – the constructor now replaces that method

PHP provides several functions to interrogate classes such as **class_exists(*class*)**, **method_exists(*class, method*)**, and **property_exists(*class, property*)** that return **TRUE** on success. You can also get a list of class members with **get_class_vars(*class*)** and **get_class_methods(*class*)** to see only "visible" members:

8 Add statements to display the total number of accessible variables in the Dog class
```
$items = get_class_vars( 'Dog' ) ;
echo '<br>Dog variables : '.count( $items ) ;
```

9 Add statements to display the names of accessible methods in the Dog class
```
echo '<br>Dog methods :' ;
$items = get_class_methods( 'Dog' ) ;
foreach( $items as $item ) { echo "$item, " ; }
```

10 Save the document in your web server's **/htdocs** directory as **constructor.php** then open the page via HTTP to see the output set by the constructor

Although the initial values of the variable members are set by the constructor, setter methods can be added to subsequently change the values – and those new values can be retrieved by the getter methods.

```
┌─────────────────────────────────────────────────┐
│ PHP Constructor      ×  +         —   □   ×       │
│ ←  →  ↻     localhost/constructor.php   ≡ ✎ ◌ ···│
├─────────────────────────────────────────────────┤
│ Fido is a brown dog                               │
│ Fido is 3 years old                               │
│ Fido weighs 15 pounds                             │
│ WOOF! WOOF!                                        │
│ ─────────────────────────────────────────────     │
│ Pooch: 4yrs 18lbs grayWOOF! WOOF!                 │
│ ─────────────────────────────────────────────     │
│ Rover: 2yrs 8lbs blackWOOF! WOOF!                 │
│                                                    │
│ Dog variables : 0                                 │
│ Dog methods :bark, __construct, __destruct, getAge, getWeight, getColor, │
│ Object Destroyed! Object Destroyed! Object Destroyed! │
└─────────────────────────────────────────────────┘
```

The number of visible variables is zero. Temporarily change their access specifier to public and see it become 3 – encapsulation in action.

Inheriting properties

A PHP class can be created as a brand new class, like those in previous examples, or can be "derived" from an existing class. Importantly, a derived class inherits members of the parent (base) class from which it is derived – in addition to its own members.

The ability to inherit members from a base class allows derived classes to be created that share certain common properties, which have been defined in the base class. For example, a "Polygon" base class may define width and height properties that are common to all polygons. Classes of "Rectangle" and Triangle" could be derived from the Polygon class – inheriting width and height properties, in addition to their own members defining their unique features.

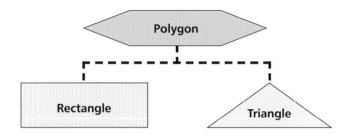

The virtue of inheritance is extremely powerful and is the second principle of Object Oriented Programming (OOP).

A derived class declaration adds the **extends** keyword after its class name, followed by the name of class from which it derives:

inheritance.php

1 Begin a PHP script by declaring a base class named "Polygon", which has two private variables initialized by the constructor, and has two public getter methods

```php
<?php
class Polygon
{
  private $width , $height ;

  function __construct( int $w = 4 , int $h = 5 )
  {
    $this->width = $w ;
    $this->height = $h ;
  }

  public function getWidth() { return $this->width ; }
  public function getHeight() { return $this->height ; }
}
```

2 After the Polygon class, declare a "Rectangle" class that derives from the Polygon class and adds a unique method

```
class Rectangle extends Polygon
{
  public function area()
  {
    return ( $this->getWidth() * $this->getHeight() ) ;
  }
}
```

3 After the Rectangle class, declare a "Triangle" class that derives from the Polygon class and adds a unique method

```
class Triangle extends Polygon
{
  public function area()
  {
    return ( $this->getWidth() * $this->getHeight() / 2 ) ;
  }
}
```

4 After the Triangle class, add two statements creating an instance of each derived class using default values

```
$rect = new Rectangle() ;
$trio = new Triangle() ;
```

105

5 Finally, add two statements to output the value returned by the unique method of each derived class

```
echo 'Rectangle Area : '.$rect->area().'<hr>' ;
echo 'Triangle Area : '.$trio->area() ;
?>
```

6 Save the document in your web server's **/htdocs** directory as **inheritance.php** then open the page via HTTP to see the output from inherited members

PHP Inheritance   ×   +

← → ↻   localhost/inheritance.php

Rectangle Area : 20

Triangle Area : 10

Embracing polymorphism

The three cornerstones of Object Oriented Programming (OOP) are encapsulation, inheritance, and polymorphism. On the previous pages we have seen how data can be encapsulated within a PHP class, and how derived classes inherit the properties of their base class, so we can now explore the final cornerstone principle of polymorphism.

The term "polymorphism" (from Greek, meaning "many forms") describes the ability to assign a different meaning or purpose to an entity according to its context. For example, in the real world everyone knows how to use a push button (entity) – you simply apply pressure to it. What that button does, however, depends on what is connected to it (context), but the result does not affect how that button is used.

In the world of Object Oriented Programming, polymorphism allows classes to have different functionality while sharing a common interface. The interface does not need to know which class it is using because they are, like the real world button, all used the same way, but can produce different contextual results. Embracing polymorphism in this way enables the programmer to create interchangeable objects that can be selected according to requirement, rather than by conditional tests.

A PHP interface is similar to a class but is declared using the **interface** keyword and can only contain method definitions, not any method statements to be executed, like this:

interface *InterfaceName*
{
  // Method definitions only go here.
}

Don't forget

Method definitions in a interface declaration may also specify parameters.

Each class that implements an interface must implement all the methods it defines by specifying their statements to be executed. A class is attached to an interface by including the **implements** keyword and interface name in its declaration, like this:

class *ClassName* implements *InterfaceName*
{
  // Method implementations go here.
}

The previous example can be modified to embrace polymorphism by adding an interface and a single function.

...cont'd

1 Rename a copy of the previous example "inheritance.php" as a new program "polymorphism.php"

polymorphism.php

2 Declare an interface named "Shape", which contains a definition for the methods already implemented in the Rectangle and Triangle classes
```
interface Shape { public function area() ; }
```

3 Edit the first line of the Rectangle and Triangle class declarations – to associate them with the interface
```
class Rectangle extends Polygon implements Shape
class Triangle extends Polygon implements Shape
```

4 After the class blocks, add a function that accepts an argument of the Shape type and calls its defined method
```
function getArea( Shape $shape )
{ return $shape->area() ; }
```

Hot tip

What's going on here?

Each call to the new **getArea()** function passes an instance object as an argument.

5 Edit the two statements creating an instance of each derived class – to pass in argument values
```
$rect = new Rectangle( 8 , 10 ) ;
$trio = new Triangle( 8 , 10 ) ;
```

The **getArea()** function calls the **area()** method defined in the interface.

6 Finally, edit the two statements to output the value returned by the unique method of each derived class, by calling each method via the interface
```
echo 'Rectangle Area : '.getArea( $rect ).'<hr>' ;
echo 'Triangle Area : '.getArea( $trio ) ;
```

The output is returned from the implementation of the **area()** method of the associated instance.

7 Save the document in your web server's **/htdocs** directory as **polymorphism.php** then open the page via HTTP to see the output via a polymorphic interface

```
☐ PHP Polymorphism    ✕  +                    —   ☐   ✕
←   →   ↻    localhost/polymorphism.php       ≡  ▨  ◌  ...

Rectangle Area : 80
─────────────────────────────────────────────
Triangle Area : 40
```

Summary

- A PHP class is a data structure that can contain both variables and functions in a single entity

- Classes are declared using the **class** keyword and can contain member variable properties and member function methods

- Access to class members from outside the class is controlled by the **public, private** or **protected** access specifier keywords

- Variable properties are encapsulated by declaring them **private** so their values can only be accessed by **public** methods

- In order to create an object you must declare an instance of a **class** data structure using the **new** keyword

- The special **->** object operator can be used to reference any visible class member

- Setter and getter methods can reference a member of the same class using the **$this** pseudo-variable

- A single setter method can assign multiple argument values, or default values, to initialize multiple variable properties

- The **_construct()** constructor method is called when a class is created and can be used to initialize variable properties

- The **_destruct()** destructor method is called when a class is destroyed and can be used to execute final statements

- PHP has functions to interrogate classes, listing methods with **get_class_methods()** and variables with **get_class_vars()**

- The three cornerstones of Object Oriented Programming are encapsulation, inheritance, and polymorphism

- A derived class declaration will include the **extends** keyword to specify a base class from which to inherit members

- An interface is declared using the **interface** keyword and the declaration may contain only method definitions

- A class is attached to an interface by including the **implements** keyword and interface name in its declaration

8 Handling files

Reading files

The ability to read and write files located on the web server is useful to log information and to provide page content. In order to process files, a "filestream" object must first be created using the PHP **fopen()** function. This requires two arguments to specify the name or path of the file and a file "mode". The file mode determines the nature of the operation to be performed and places the file pointer at a suitable position within the file:

File mode:	Operation:
r	Open an existing file to read File pointer starts at the beginning of the file
w	Discard all contents of an existing file or create a new file if none exists File pointer starts at the beginning of the file
a	Open an existing file and preserve all contents File pointer starts at the end of the file
r+	Open a file to read from or write to File pointer starts at the beginning of the file
w+	Open a file to write to or read from Discard all contents of an existing file or create a new file if none exists File pointer starts at the beginning of the file
a+	Open a file to read from or write to and preserve all contents File pointer starts at the end of the file

It is good practice to always provide an alternative with the **die()** function in case the attempt to create a filestream fails.

When a filestream is created successfully, the file can be read by specifying the filestream and byte size as arguments to the **fread()** function. If the whole file is to be read it is convenient to use the **filesize()** function to specify the byte size of the file to be read.

Upon completion of any file operation, the filestream must be destroyed by specifying it as an argument to the **fclose()** function.

Beware

The file mode specifier must appear within quote marks when supplied as an argument to the **fopen()** function.

Hot tip

Specify an explanatory message as an argument to the **die()** function.

...cont'd

```
manifesto.txt - Notepad                                    —    □    ×
File  Edit  Format  View  Help
The workers have nothing to lose in this [revolution] but their chains.
They have a world to gain.
Workers of the world unite!

- Karl Marx , The Communist Manifesto 1848
```

1 Begin a PHP script with statements that attempt to open
a plain text file for reading, or exit the script upon failure
```php
<?php
$filestream = fopen( 'manifesto.txt' , 'r' )
or die( 'Unable to open file!' ) ;
```

read.php

2 Next, add a statement to read the text file upon success
and display its entire contents
```php
echo fread( $filestream , filesize( 'manifesto.txt' ) ) ;
```

3 Now, remember to close the file stream
```php
fclose( $filestream ) ;
```

4 Save the document in your web server's **/htdocs** directory
as **read.php**, alongside the plain text file to be read, then
open the page via HTTP to see the text file contents
displayed in the browser window

Unlike a PHP block within
an HTML document, a
purely PHP script needs
no closing **?>** tag.

```
localhost                    ×   +              —    □    ×
←  →  ○        localhost/read.php         ≡  📝  ◌  ...

The workers have nothing to lose in this [revolution] but their chains. They
have a world to gain. Workers of the world unite! - Karl Marx , The
Communist Manifesto 1848
```

Notice that the output
here does not maintain
line endings – but the
example overleaf does.

Reading lines

Once a "filestream" object is created, its contents can be read one line at a time by specifying the filestream as an argument to the PHP **fgets()** function. To read every line this function can be called repeatedly in a loop. The **feof()** function can determine when the end of the file is reached and can end the loop:

The **feof()** function returns true when the end of the file is reached.

```
manifesto.txt - Notepad                                    —    □    ×
File  Edit  Format  View  Help
The workers have nothing to lose in this [revolution] but their chains.
They have a world to gain.
Workers of the world unite!

- Karl Marx , The Communist Manifesto 1848
```

readlines.php

1 Begin a PHP script with statements that attempt to open a plain text file for reading, or exit the script upon failure
```php
<?php
$fllestream = fopen( 'manifesto.txt' , 'r' )
or die( 'Unable to open file!' ) ;
```

2 Next, add a loop to read the text file line-by-line upon success and display its entire contents
```php
while( !feof( $filestream ) )
{ echo fgets( $filestream ).'<br>' ; }
```

The next to last line is not actually empty – it contains an invisible newline character.

3 Now, remember to close the file stream
```php
fclose( $filestream ) ;
```

4 Save the document in your web server's **/htdocs** directory as **readlines.php**, alongside the plain text file to be read, then open the page via HTTP to see the text file lines

```
□ localhost              ×   +                          —    □    ×
←   →   ↻        localhost/readlines.php          ≡   🗒   ◌   ...

The workers have nothing to lose in this [revolution] but their chains.
They have a world to gain.
Workers of the world unite!

- Karl Marx , The Communist Manifesto 1848
```

Reading characters

Once a "filestream" object is created, its contents can be read one character at a time by specifying the filestream as an argument to the PHP **fgetc()** function. To read every character this function can be called repeatedly in a loop. The **fgetc()** function will return false when the end of the file is reached and can end the loop:

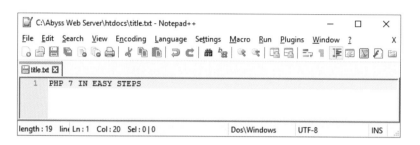

If you create this text file using Windows' Notepad app you will see leading Byte Order Mark characters in this example. The Notepad++ app shown here does not add these.

1 Begin a PHP script with statements that attempt to open a plain text file for reading, or exit the script upon failure
```php
<?php
$filestream = fopen( 'title.txt' , 'r' )
or die( 'Unable to open file!' ) ;
```

readchars.php

2 Next, add a loop to read the text file character-by-character upon success and display its entire contents
```php
while( $char = fgetc( $filestream ) )
{ echo $char.' * ' ; }
```

3 Now, remember to close the file stream
```php
fclose( $filestream ) ;
```

4 Save the document in your web server's **/htdocs** directory as **readchars.php**, alongside the plain text file to be read, then open the page via HTTP to see the file characters

The **fgetc()** function returns false when there are no more characters to get from the stream.

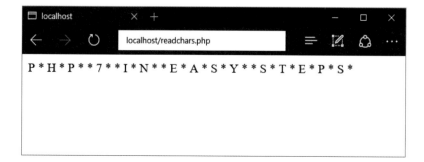

Writing a file

Once a "filestream" object has been created specifying a write mode, a text file can be created. Text can be written into the file by specifying the filestream and a file name to the PHP **fwrite()** function. To format the text, non-printing invisible characters can also be written to create line breaks and tab spacing:

Character:	Description:
\n	Newline Move to a new line down
\r	Carriage return Move to the beginning of the line
\t	Tab Move along the line to the next tab stop

Beware

Strings containing non-printing characters must be enclosed within double quotes so that PHP can interpret them.

PHP

write.php

1 Begin a PHP script with a statement to assign text, including non-printing characters for formatting
```php
<?php
$poem = "\r\n\tI never saw a man who looked" ;
$poem .= "\r\n\tWith such a wistful eye" ;
$poem .= "\r\n\tUpon that little tent of blue" ;
$poem .= "\r\n\tWhich prisoners call the sky" ;
```

2 Next, assign a name for the file to be written
```php
$filename = 'poem.txt' ;
```

3 Attempt to create a plain text file for writing, or exit the script upon failure
```php
$filestream = fopen( $filename , 'w' )
or die( 'Unable to open file!' ) ;
```

4 Write the file and display a confirmation of how many bytes have been written in total
```php
$num = fwrite( $filestream , $poem ) ;
if( $num )
{
  echo "$num bytes written to $filename" ;
}
```

5 Now, remember to close the file stream
```php
fclose( $filestream ) ;
```

...cont'd

6 Save the document in your web server's **/htdocs** directory as **write.php** then open the page via HTTP to see confirmation that the text file has been written

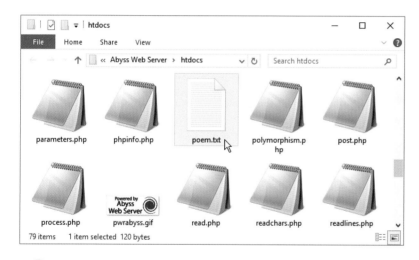

7 Use File Explorer to navigate to your web server's **/htdocs** directory and see the file created by the PHP script

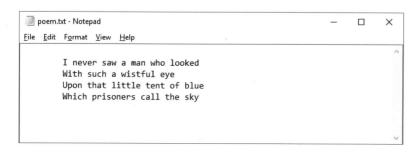

8 Open the file to see the text written by the PHP script

Hot tip

You can run this example repeatedly and each time it will erase the content then write it again.

Appending text

Once a "filestream" object has been created specifying an append mode, a text file can be opened to add text at its end. Text can be appended to the file by specifying the filestream and a file name to the PHP **fwrite()** function. The process is identical to writing a file, except that the file pointer is positioned at the end of existing content before the text is written into the file:

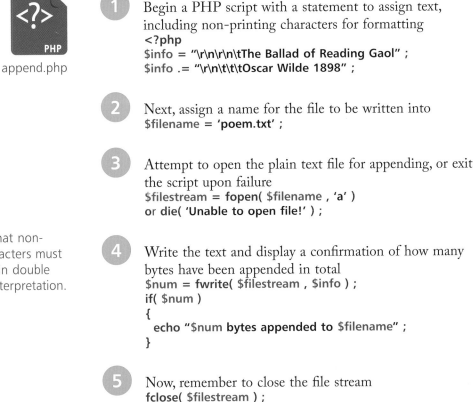

append.php

Remember that non-printing characters must be enclosed in double quotes for interpretation.

1. Begin a PHP script with a statement to assign text, including non-printing characters for formatting
```
<?php
$info = "\r\n\r\n\tThe Ballad of Reading Gaol" ;
$info .= "\r\n\t\t\tOscar Wilde 1898" ;
```

2. Next, assign a name for the file to be written into
```
$filename = 'poem.txt' ;
```

3. Attempt to open the plain text file for appending, or exit the script upon failure
```
$filestream = fopen( $filename , 'a' )
or die( 'Unable to open file!' ) ;
```

4. Write the text and display a confirmation of how many bytes have been appended in total
```
$num = fwrite( $filestream , $info ) ;
if( $num )
{
  echo "$num bytes appended to $filename" ;
}
```

5. Now, remember to close the file stream
```
fclose( $filestream ) ;
```

6. Save the document in your web server's **/htdocs** directory as **append.php** then open the page via HTTP to see confirmation that the text has been appended to the file

52 bytes appended to poem.txt

...cont'd

7 Navigate to your web server's **/htdocs** directory and open the file to see the text appended by the PHP script

```
poem.txt - Notepad                              —   □   ×
File  Edit  Format  View  Help

        I never saw a man who looked
        With such a wistful eye
        Upon that little tent of blue
        Which prisoners call the sky

        The Ballad of Reading Gaol
                    Oscar Wilde 1898
```

Overwriting text

It is important to recognize that when you write to an existing file in write mode it will overwrite any existing content:

1 Begin a PHP script by attempting to open an existing text file for writing, or exit the script upon failure
```php
<?php
$filestream = fopen( 'poem.txt' , 'w' )
or die( 'Unable to open file!' ) ;
```

overwrite.php

2 Upon success, write new text into the file
```php
fwrite( $filestream , 'Overwritten!' ) ;
```

3 Now, remember to close the file stream
```php
fclose( $filestream ) ;
```

4 Save the document in your web server's **/htdocs** directory as **overwrite.php** then open the page via HTTP and reopen the text file to see its contents overwritten

Be careful when writing to files as it is easy to accidentally overwrite.

```
poem.txt - Notepad                              —   □   ×
File  Edit  Format  View  Help
Overwritten!
```

Handling errors

You can anticipate possible errors and terminate a running script when they occur using the **die()** function or the **exit()** function. Without this contingency the default PHP error handler provides a useful, but unsightly message when an error occurs. For example, **fopen('nonsuch.txt' , 'r')** to open a non-existing file:

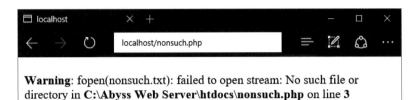

It is not always desirable to terminate a script when an error occurs, but you can create a custom error handler to provide a more user-friendly message than that provided by the default PHP error handler. A custom error handler is simply a function with this syntax:

function error_handler(*level* , *message* , *file* , *line* , *context*)

Only the first two parameters are required, the rest are optional. The first of these is a numerical value, representing a constant, indicating the severity of the error that has occurred:

Level:	Constant:	Description:
2	E_WARNING	Non-fatal runtime error
8	E_NOTICE	Non-fatal possible error
256	E_USER_ERROR	Fatal user-generated error
512	E_USER_WARNING	Non-fatal user-generated error

A custom error handler function is nominated to handle errors by specifying its function name as the argument to the built-in PHP **set_error_handler()** function.

The error handler is called when an error occurs, or can be called explicitly using the **trigger_error()** function to specify an error message as its argument.

The **die()** and **exit()** functions perform identical operations in PHP, but their terminology can have different appeals. For some, **die()** possibly seems more appropriate to quit when an error is detected, and **exit()** may seem more suitable to quit in other scenarios.

The basic error levels are listed in this table but the PHP manual lists many more (**php.net/ manual**).

1 Begin a PHP script by defining a custom error handler function to report an error level and error message

```php
<?php
function error_handler( $level , $message )
{
  switch( $level )
  {
    case 2  : $str = 'Warning!' ;   break ;
    case 8  : $str = 'Notice!' ;    break ;
    default : $str = 'Error!' ;
  }
  echo "<b>$str</b><br>$message<hr>";
}
```

error.php

2 Next, nominate the function to handle errors

```php
set_error_handler( 'error_handler' ) ;
```

3 Now, for some mischief – attempt to access an uninitialized variable and try to open a non-existing file

```php
echo( $var ) ;
$file = fopen( 'nonsuch.txt' , 'r' ) ;
```

4 Explicitly trigger the custom error handler

```php
$number = 2 ;
if( $number >= 1 )
{
  trigger_error( 'Value of number must be 1 or less' ) ;
}
```

Notice that the script continues after reporting each error, it does not terminate on error.

5 Save the document in your web server's **/htdocs** directory as **error.php** then open the page via HTTP to see the error levels and appropriate messages

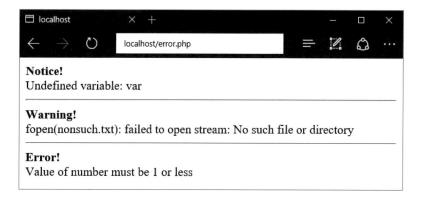

Notice!
Undefined variable: var

Warning!
fopen(nonsuch.txt): failed to open stream: No such file or directory

Error!
Value of number must be 1 or less

Catching exceptions

We can choose how a script should proceed when a specific error condition occurs. This error condition is called an "exception". When an exception occurs it is said to be "thrown", and code handling the exception is said to be its "catch". If an exception is not caught, PHP will treat it as a fatal error and issue an unsightly "Uncaught Exception" message, something like this:

Fatal error: Uncaught Exception: Number : 5 Value must exceed 10 in C:\Abyss Web Server\htdocs\uncaught.php:9 Stack trace: #0 C:\Abyss Web Server\htdocs\uncaught.php(13): check_size(5) #1 {main} thrown in **C:\Abyss Web Server\htdocs\uncaught.php** on line **9**

Beware

Each **try** block must have an associated **catch** block, otherwise a fatal Uncaught Exception error will occur.

The key to handling exceptions is to anticipate the error by trying to execute an action within a **try** code block, and determine how the script should proceed in an associated **catch** code block. The catching block is passed an **Exception** class object that has **getMessage()**, **getFile()** and **getLine()** methods to retrieve details.

An instance of the **Exception** class can be created using the **new** keyword, and can be explicitly thrown using the **throw** keyword.

A custom exception handler can also be created as a derived class of the **Exception** class, to provide your own custom methods:

exception.php

1 Begin a PHP script by defining a function that will throw an exception when a conditional test fails

```php
<?php
function check_size( $num )
{
  if( $num < 10 )
  { throw new
    Exception( "Number : $num<br>Value must exceed 10" ) ; }
}
```

2 Anticipate a specific error and report the exception

```php
try { check_size( 5 ) ; }
catch( Exception $e )
{       echo '<b>Size Exception!</b><br>'.
        $e->getMessage().'<hr>' ;              }
```

3 Next, create a custom exception handler class

```
class CustomException extends Exception
{
  public function get_details()
  {
    $details = 'File : '.$this->getFile().
    '<br>Line : '.$this->getLine().
    '<br>'.$this->getMessage() ;
    return $details ;
  }
}
```

Don't forget

For more on derived classes and inheritance see page 102.

4 Now, add another function that will throw an exception when a conditional test fails

```
function check_parity( $num )
{
  if( $num % 2 !== 0 )
  {
    throw new CustomException( "Number :
                $num<br>Value must be even" ) ;
  }
}
```

5 Finally, anticipate a specific error and report the exception

```
try { check_parity( 5 ) ; }
catch( CustomException $e )
{  echo '<b>Parity Exception!</b><br>'.
       $e->get_details().'<hr>' ;              }
```

6 Save the document in your web server's **/htdocs** directory as **exception.php** then open the page via HTTP to see the exceptions caught and appropriate message details

Hot tip

A **try** block can contain multiple **throw** statements to anticipate multiple error conditions, and can be followed by multiple **catch** blocks to handle those exceptions.

Summary

- The **fopen()** function is used to create a filestream object and requires two arguments to specify a file name and a file mode

- It is good practice to provide an alternative with the **die()** function in case an attempt to create a filestream fails

- The **fread()** function is used to read a filestream created using the 'r' file mode, and the **filesize()** function can be used to specify the byte size of the file

- Upon completion of any file operation the filestream must be destroyed by calling the **fclose()** function

- The **fgets()** function can be used to read a file line-by-line and the **feof()** function can recognize the end of a file

- The **fgetc()** function can be used to read a file character-by-character and will return false at the end of the file

- Text can be written into a file by specifying the filestream and the file name as arguments to the **fwrite()** function

- The **fwrite()** function will overwrite existing text using the 'w' file mode but will append text when using the 'a' file mode

- The name of a function can be specified as the argument to the **set_error_handler()** function to nominate it as a custom error handler

- The error handler function is called when an error occurs or can be called explicitly using the **trigger_error()** function

- An exception is thrown when a specific error condition occurs

- If an exception is not caught, PHP will treat it as a fatal error and issue an Uncaught Exception message

- A **try** code block is used to anticipate a specific error and its associated **catch** block is used to determine how the script should proceed when that error occurs

- An **Exception** class object has **getMessage()**, **getFile()** and **getLine()** methods that can retrieve exception details

- A custom exception handler can be created as a derived class of the **Exception** class to provide custom exception methods

9 Producing forms

Performing actions

Processing data submitted from an HTML form on a web page is perhaps the most fundamental task performed by a PHP script.

The HTML **<form>** tag's **action** attribute is used to nominate the PHP script that will process ("handle") the form data. Additionally, the **<form>** tag's **method** attribute is used to specify how the data is sent to the script – typically by the **POST** method. So the HTML form tag and attributes might look like this:

<form action="script.php" method="POST">

PHP provides a special "superglobal" **$_POST** array variable in which it stores form data submitted by the **POST** method. It creates an array element of the same name as each submitted form element name, storing the value they contain. For example with this form element:

<input type="text" name="email" >

On submission of the form, PHP will create an array element named **$_POST['email']** containing the value entered into that form input by the user.

For easy recognition PHP variables of the same names as the form elements can be assigned the values stored in their corresponding **$_POST** array elements. The values can then be displayed in a response page created by the action handler script:

Beware

This is case-sensitive so the capitalization must be precisely as described – **$_POST['EMail']** or **$_Post['email']** are incorrect for example.

PHP

action.php

 1 Create an HTML document containing a form with three text input fields for data submission
```
<form action="action_handler.php" method="POST">
<dl>
<dt>Name:
<dd><input type="text" name="name">
<dt>Email Address:
<dd><input type="text" name="mail">
<dt>Comments:
<dd><textarea rows="5" cols="20" name="comment" >
</textarea>
</dl>
<p><input type="submit" ></p>
</form>
```

 2 Now, save the document in your web server's **/htdocs** directory as **action.php**

3 Next create an HTML document containing a script to assign form values to like-named PHP variables for output

```php
<?php
$name = $_POST['name'] ;
$mail = $_POST['mail'] ;
$comment = $_POST['comment'] ;
echo "<p>Thanks for this comment $name ...</p>" ;
echo "<p><i>$comment</i></p>" ;
echo "<p>We will reply to $mail</p>" ;
?>
```

action_handler.php

4 Save the document in your web server's **/htdocs** directory as **action_handler.php** then open **action.php** via HTTP and submit some data to see it get displayed in the response page produced by the PHP script

Hot tip

Form submission methods may be either "GET" or "POST". The **GET** method appends name=value pairs to the URL but is mostly used to request information – such as retrieving a database record. The **POST** method can submit more data, is more secure as the data is not appended to the URL, and is mostly used when an action is to be performed – such as updating a database record. The **POST** method is therefore preferred for most examples in this book.

Checking set values

PHP can easily ensure that the user has entered data into submitted HTML form fields using the built-in **isset()** function. This function takes the name of a variable as its argument and returns **TRUE** only if that variable value is not **NULL** – thus ensuring that the variable has been "set" with some value. Empty form fields will be **NULL** unless the user has entered a value.

Conditional tests can be made with the **isset()** function to indicate where form fields have been left empty, or to provide a response page where the fields have been completed:

isset.php

1 Create an HTML document containing a form with three radio buttons providing a single field for data submission

```
<form action="isset_handler.php" method="POST">
<fieldset>
<legend>What kind of language is PHP?</legend>
Scripting<input type="radio"
        name="definition" value="Scripting"> <br>
Markup<input type="radio"
        name="definition" value="Markup"> <br>
Programming<input type="radio"
        name="definition" value="Programming">
</fieldset><p><input type="submit" ></p>
</form>
```

2 Now, save the document in your web server's **/htdocs** directory as **isset.php**

isset_handler.php

3 Next, create an HTML document containing a PHP script to initialize a variable with a submitted value – or with **NULL** if no value has been submitted

```
<?php

if ( isset( $_POST['definition'] ) )
{
  $definition = $_POST['definition'] ;
}
else
{
  $definition = NULL ;
}

# Response statements to be inserted here (step 4).

?>
```

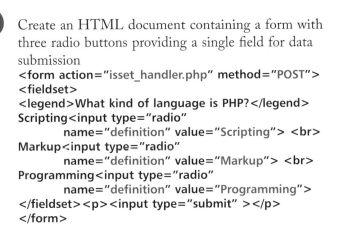

4 Finally, insert statements to output an appropriate response according to the value of the variable

```
if ( $definition != NULL )
{
  if ( $definition != 'Scripting' )
  { echo "$definition is Incorrect" ; }
  else
  { echo "$definition is Correct" ; }
}
else
{ echo 'You must select one answer' ; }
?>
```

Hot tip

It is technically more efficient to test whether a condition is not **TRUE** than whether it is **TRUE** – as fewer possibilities need evaluating.

5 Save the document in your web server's **/htdocs** directory as **isset_handler.php** then open **isset.php** via HTTP and submit the form to see the responses

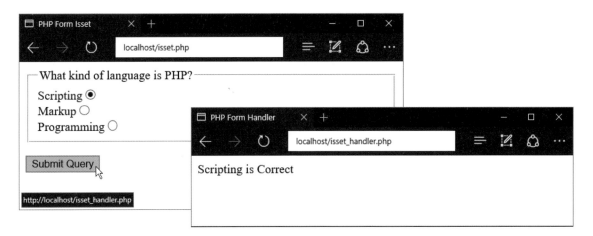

Validating form data

As users may inadvertently submit forms with empty fields, or with data in the wrong format, it is essential your PHP scripts ensure required fields are completed and submitted data is valid.

To ensure the user has entered something into a text field, PHP provides an **empty()** function that accepts a variable argument and returns **TRUE** if its value is an empty string, zero, **NULL** or **FALSE**.

To ensure the user has entered data in numeric format, PHP provides an **is_numeric()** function that accepts a variable argument and returns **TRUE** only if its value is a number.

More specific data validation can be performed using the PHP **preg_match()** function that accepts a "regular expression" argument and a variable argument in which to seek a pattern. Typically, this is used to ensure an email address is in the expected format:

valid.php

 Create an HTML document containing a form with two text fields for data submission
```
<form action="valid_handler.php" method="POST">
<fieldset>
<legend>Enter a quantity and email address</legend>
<p>Quantity : <input type="text" name="quantity"></p>
<p>Email Address : <input type="text" name="email"></p>
</fieldset><p><input type="submit" ></p>
</form>
```

2 Now, save the document in your web server's **/htdocs** directory as **valid.php**

valid_handler.php

3 Next, create an HTML document containing a PHP script to initialize a variable with a submitted value – or with **NULL** if no value has been submitted
```
<?php
if ( !empty ( $_POST['quantity'] ) )
{
  $quantity = $_POST['quantity'] ;
  # Format validation to be inserted here (step 4).
}
else
{ $quantity = NULL ; echo 'You must enter a quantity<br>' ; }
```

4 Insert statements to ensure the format is numeric
```
if ( !is_numeric( $quantity ) )
{ $quantity = NULL ; echo 'Quantity must be numeric<br>' ; }
```

5 Now, add statements to initialize another variable with a submitted value – or with **NULL** if no value is submitted

```
if ( !empty ( $_POST['email'] ) )
{
  $email = $_POST['email'] ;
  # Format validation to be inserted here (step 6).
}
else
{ $email = NULL ; echo 'You must enter an email address' ; }
```

6 Next, insert statements to ensure the email address uses the expected pattern

```
$pattern = '/\b[\w.-]+@[\w.-]+\.[A-Za-z]{2,6}\b/' ;
if ( !preg_match( $pattern , $email ) )
{ $email = NULL ; echo 'Email address is incorrect format' ; }
```

7 Finally, add a statement to output valid submitted data

```
 if ( ( $quantity != NULL ) && ( $email != NULL ) )
{ echo "Email : $email<br>Quantity : $quantity " ; }
?>
```

8 Save the document in your web server's **/htdocs** directory as **valid_handler.php** then open **valid.php** via HTTP and submit the form to see the responses

Hot tip

Strictly speaking, the topic of regular expressions is outside the remit of this book, but you can precisely copy the pattern in this example to ensure email addresses are in the expected format.

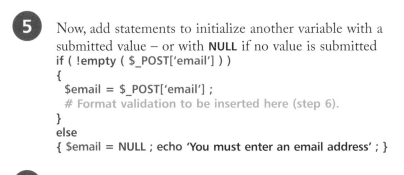

Filtering data

To validate user input easily, PHP provides a **filter_var()** function that can be used to both validate and "sanitize" input values. This function requires two arguments to specify the variable to be filtered and a constant name of the filter to be used:

Filter Constant Name:	Convention:
FILTER_VALIDATE_BOOLEAN	Boolean value
FILTER_VALIDATE_EMAIL	Email address format
FILTER_VALIDATE_FLOAT	Floating-point number
FILTER_VALIDATE_INT	Integer number
FILTER_VALIDATE_IP	IP address format
FILTER_VALIDATE_MAC	MAC address format
FILTER_VALIDATE_REGEXP	Regular expression format
FILTER_VALIDATE_URL	URL format
FILTER_SANITIZE_EMAIL	Strip invalid characters
FILTER_SANITIZE_ENCODED	URL-encode string
FILTER_SANITIZE_MAGIC_QUOTES	Backslash-escape characters
FILTER_SANITIZE_NUMBER_FLOAT	Strip all non-digits
FILTER_SANITIZE_NUMBER_INT	Strip all non-digits
FILTER_SANITIZE_SPECIAL_CHARS	HTML-escape '"<>&
FILTER_SANITIZE_STRING	Strip HTML tags
FILTER_SANITIZE_URL	Strip invalid characters
FILTER_CALLBACK	Call a custom filter function

The validation filters return **TRUE** when validation succeeds, otherwise they will return **FALSE**.

Some filters allow further options to be specified. For example, a numeric range can be specified to **FILTER_VALIDATE_INT**.

filter.php

1 Create an HTML document containing a PHP script that begins by writing a styled HTML page heading
```php
<?php
$hdr = '<h1 style="color:red">PHP in easy steps</h1>' ;
echo $hdr ;
```

2 Next, sanitize the page heading by stripping the HTML tags to remove styling and display the stripped version
```php
$hdr = filter_var( $hdr , FILTER_SANITIZE_STRING ) ;
echo "Sanitized heading : $hdr" ;
```

3 Now, add a function to validate a parameter as being a correctly formatted email address
```php
function validate( $email )
{
  if ( filter_var( $email , FILTER_VALIDATE_EMAIL ) )
  { echo( "<hr>$email IS a valid email address" ) ; }
  else
  { echo( "<hr>$email IS NOT a valid email address" ); }
}
```

4 Create an email address containing an illegal space and attempt validation, then sanitize the email address and attempt validation once more
```php
$email = 'mike @example.com' ;
validate( $email ) ;
$email = filter_var( $email , FILTER_SANITIZE_EMAIL ) ;
validate( $email ) ;
?>
```

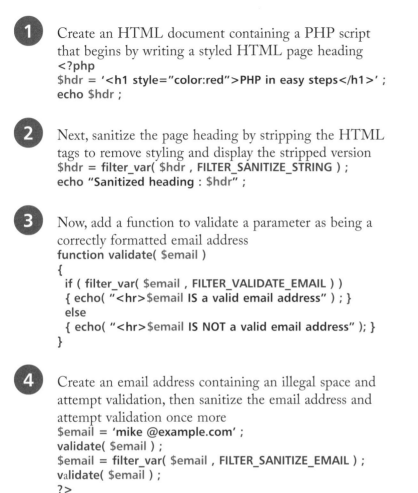

Submitted user input can break your webpage so should always be validated.

5 Save the document in your web server's **/htdocs** directory as **filter.php** then open it via HTTP to see filtration

PHP in easy steps

Sanitized heading : PHP in easy steps

mike @example.com IS NOT a valid email address

mike@example.com IS a valid email address

Sending hidden data

In addition to data entered by the user into HTML form input fields, data generated by PHP can be submitted using HTML hidden form fields. Like regular input fields these also send a name=value pair to the form handler script, but here the value is supplied by PHP, not by the user.

Typically, data submitted using hidden form fields might include the login name of the user and a timestamp of the submission:

hidden.php

The timestamp in this example is created when the form gets created, not when the form gets submitted.

1 Create an HTML document containing a PHP script to define the timezone and initialize two variables

```php
<?php
date_default_timezone_set( 'UTC' ) ;
$time = date( ' H:i , F j ' ) ;
$user = 'Mike' ;
```

2 Now, add a statement to write a complete form containing a regular input field and two hidden fields, whose values are set by the variables

```php
echo '
<form action="hidden_handler.php" method="POST">
<fieldset>
<legend>Send us your comments</legend>
<textarea rows="5" cols="20" name="comment">
</textarea>
<input type="hidden" name="user" value=" '. $user .' ">
<input type="hidden" name="time" value=" '. $time.' ">
</fieldset><p><input type="submit" ></p></form> ' ;
?>
```

3 Save the document in your web server's **/htdocs** directory as **hidden.php**

hidden_handler.php

4 Next, create an HTML document containing a PHP script to initialize a variable with a submitted value – or with **NULL** if no value has been submitted

```php
<?php
if ( !empty ( $_POST['comment'] ) )
{
  $comment = $_POST['comment'] ;
}
else
{
  $comment = NULL ; echo 'You must enter a comment' ;
}
```

...cont'd

5 Now, add statements to initialize two variables if the hidden form field values have been set
```
$time =
( !isset ( $_POST['time'] ) ) ? NULL : $_POST['time'] ;

$user =
( !isset ( $_POST['user'] ) ) ? NULL : $_POST['user'] ;
```

6 Finally, add a statement to output valid submitted data
```
if ( ( $comment != NULL )  &&
                ( $time != NULL ) && ( $user != NULL )  )
{ echo "<p>Comment received : \" $comment \"<br>
                        From $user at $time </p>" ; }

?>
```

7 Save the document in your web server's **/htdocs** directory as **hidden_handler.php** then open **hidden.php** via HTTP and submit the form to see the responses

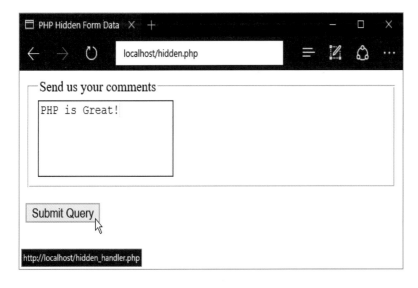

Hot tip

Notice the ternary ? : operator is used here in place of a more lengthy **if else** statement.

Don't forget

You can include quotes in output by prefixing them with a backslash to escape them from recognition – as demonstrated here.

Handling submissions

The examples so far in this chapter have each used two documents – one to display an HTML form and another to handle the form submission. This procedure can however be performed by a single document, using a simple technique to determine whether a form should be displayed or its submission should be handled.

PHP provides a special "superglobal" **$_SERVER** array variable with a **REQUEST_METHOD** element in which it stores the type of request. Where a form uses the **POST** method for submission, two different types of request are made to the PHP script when the page loads – simply displaying the form uses the standard **GET** method made by most web pages, whereas submitting the form uses the **POST** method. Therefore the request method can be examined to determine which course of action to take.

Using this technique, the name of the same single page is also specified as the form handler to the HTML **action** attribute. The form can be displayed by the usual **echo** instruction and validation checks can be made for the response in the same way as described for separate form handler scripts:

single.php

 Create an HTML document containing a PHP script that examines the page request method

```php
<?php
if ( $_SERVER[ 'REQUEST_METHOD' ] != 'POST' )
{
  # Form display statements to be inserted here (step 2).
}
else
{
  # Form handling statements to be inserted here(step 3).
}
```

2 Now, insert a statement to display a form when the page has been requested by the standard **GET** method

```php
 echo '
<form action="single.php" method="POST">
<fieldset>
<legend>Send us your comments</legend>
<textarea rows="5" cols="40" name="comment">
</textarea>
</fieldset>
<p><input type="submit" ></p>
</form> ' ;
```

3 Next, insert a statement to handle the form submission
when the page has been requested by the **POST** method

```
if ( !empty ( $_POST['comment'] ) )
{
  $comment = $_POST['comment'] ;
  echo "Comment : $comment " ;
}
else
{ $comment = NULL ; echo 'You must enter a comment' ; }
?>
```

Hot tip

The form will be handled
by the same page on
submission if the action
attribute specifies an
empty string **action=""**
– but it is preferable to
specify the page name.

4 Save the document in your web server's **/htdocs** directory as
single.php then submit the form to see the responses

Making sticky forms

When a user attempts to submit a form where a required field has not been completed, it is desirable to retain the entries in the fields they have completed, by making the form "sticky". This is especially so for lengthy forms with many fields – so the user need not complete all fields once more – and is easily achieved with PHP.

Simply assigning the relevant submitted field data from the **$_POST** array to the HTML tag's **value** attribute with **echo** retains the entry when the form is displayed again for completion. As a precaution, the statement should use the **isset()** function to check that the field was in fact completed before submission.

An error message for each incomplete field can be assigned to an array to advise of omissions when the form is displayed again, or a message written confirming success when all fields are completed:

sticky.php

Hot tip

$_SERVER['PHP_SELF'] is used by this example to ensure the script will still work if renamed.

Don't forget

The **if** statement tests that the form has been submitted by checking the request method is **POST**, not the **GET** method that is used to display the empty form.

 1 Create an HTML document containing a sticky form with two text fields for name and email address details

```
<form method="POST"
        action="<?php $_SERVER[ 'PHP_SELF' ] ?>" >
<p>Name:
<input type="text" name="name"
        value="<?php if ( isset( $_POST[ 'name' ] ) )
                echo $_POST[ 'name' ] ; ?>"> </p>
<p>Email:
<input type="text" name="email"
        value="<?php if ( isset( $_POST[ 'email' ] ) )
                echo $_POST[ 'email' ] ; ?>"></p>
<p><input type="submit"></p>
</form>
```

2 Now, add a PHP script to handle the form submission

```
<?php

if ( $_SERVER[ 'REQUEST_METHOD' ] == 'POST' )
{
  // Statements to be inserted here (steps 3-5).
}

?>
```

3 Next, insert into the PHP script block a statement to create an array for error messages

```
$errors = array() ;
```

...cont'd

4 Then, insert statements to initialize variables with submitted values, or add to the errors array for omissions
if (empty($_POST['name'])) { $errors[] = 'name' ; }
else { $name = trim($_POST['name']) ; }

if (empty($_POST['email'])) { $errors[] = 'email' ; }
else { $email = trim($_POST['email']) ; }

5 Now, insert statements to write error messages or confirm successful form submission
if(!empty($errors))
{ echo 'Error! Please enter your ' ;
  foreach ($errors as $msg) { echo " - $msg " ; } }
else { echo "Success! Thanks $name " ; }

6 Save the document in your web server's **/htdocs** directory as **sticky.php** then open it via HTTP and submit the form to see the retained values and response messages

It is good practice to use the **trim()** function, as seen here, to remove any leading and trailing spaces from the submitted field value.

Uploading files

The PHP **$_FILES** superglobal variable makes it simple to **POST** file uploads from an HTML form if the **<form>** tag includes an **enctype** attribute set to "multipart/formdata". When submitted, a **$_FILES** associative array is created with keys that include the file **name**, a generated temporary name (**tmp_name**), and the file **size**. The file name and size can be used for validation. The temporary filename can then be specified to the **move_uploaded_file()** function along with the original filename to upload the file:

upload.php

1 Create an HTML document containing a sticky form with a file type input named "image"

```
<form action="<?php $_SERVER[ 'PHP_SELF' ] ?>"
    method="POST"  enctype = "multipart/formdata" >
Select an image to upload :
<input type="file" name="image" >
<input type="submit" value="Upload Image"> </form>
```

2 Now add a PHP script to handle the form submission

```
<?php

if ( $_SERVER[ 'REQUEST_METHOD' ] == 'POST' )
{
    // Statements to be inserted here (steps 3-7).
}

?>
```

Beware

The PHP configuration must permit file uploads for this example to work. The configuration file **php.ini**, within the PHP directory, must contain a line **file_uploads = On**.

3 Next, insert statements to initialize three variables with information about the file selected by the user

```
$name = $_FILES[ 'image' ][ 'name' ] ;
$temp = $_FILES[ 'image' ][ 'tmp_name' ] ;
$size = $_FILES[ 'image' ][ 'size' ] ;
```

4 Now, insert statements to ensure the selected file is of a desired file type by testing the file extension, or quit

```
$ext = pathinfo( $name , PATHINFO_EXTENSION ) ;
$ext = strtolower( $ext ) ;
if( $ext != 'png' && $ext != 'jpg' && $ext != 'gif' )
{ echo 'Format must be PNG, JPG, or GIF' ; exit() ; }
```

Hot tip

Notice how the **pathinfo()** function provides the file extension part of the filename here.

5 Insert a statement to ensure the selected file is of a desired file size, or quit

```
if( $size > 512000 )
{ echo 'File size must not exceed 500Kb' ; exit() ; }
```

6 Insert a statement to ensure the selected file does not have the same name as one already on the server, or quit
```
if( file_exists( $name ) )
{ echo 'File '.$name.' already uploaded' ; exit() ; }
```

7 Finally, attempt to upload the file, naming it by its original filename and displaying it below the form
```
try
{
  move_uploaded_file( $temp , $name ) ;
  echo 'File uploaded : '.$name ;
  echo '<br><img src="'.$name.'">' ;
}
catch( Exception $e )
{
  echo 'File upload failed!' ;
}
```

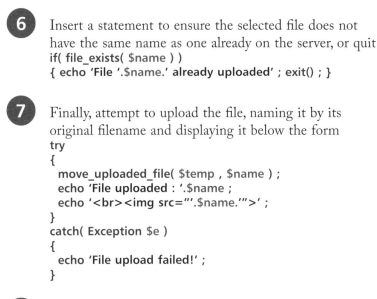

Hot tip

The arguments to the **move_uploaded_file()** function specify the (temporary) filename and destination. It could usefully specify a dedicated directory path destination, such as **'uploads/'.$name**.

8 Save the document in your web server's **/htdocs** directory as **upload.php** then open it via HTTP and select a suitable image file for upload to the **/htdocs** directory

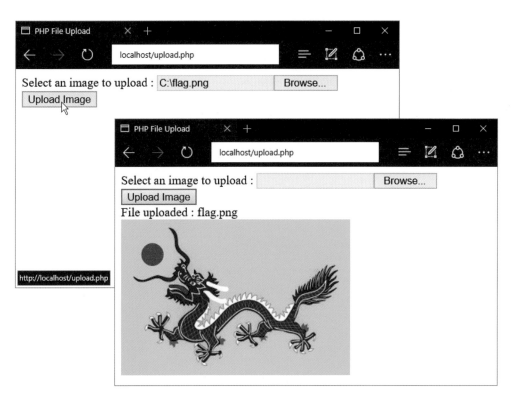

Surrounding forms

PHP usefully allows multiple files to be incorporated together to create a single web page. This means that dynamic forms can be surrounded by static header and footer content that can be easily re-used to create other pages within a website.

The PHP **include()** function takes the URL of another file to be incorporated within a web page as its argument. Typically, included static content files are HTML and are located in an "includes" folder within the **/htdocs** directory of your web server.

PHP also provides a **require()** function that works just like the **include()** function to incorporate other files within a web page, but is subtly different. When the **include()** function fails, as the specified file cannot be found for example, a warning gets sent to the browser but the script continues to run. When the **require()** function fails an error is printed but the script gets halted. Usually the **include()** function incorporates static HTML files, whereas the **require()** function incorporates dynamic PHP scripts.

Importantly, the title of a web page incorporating multiple files can be dynamically written by PHP to allow maximum flexibility of otherwise static HTML header content:

header.html

 Create an HTML document containing static header content and a PHP snippet to write the page title

```
<!DOCTYPE HTML>
<html lang="en">
<head>
<meta charset="UTF-8">
<title> <?php echo $page_title ; ?> </title>
<link rel="stylesheet" href="includes/style.css">
</head>

<body>
<header><h1>Page Header</h1></header>
```

footer.html

2 Now, create an HTML document containing footer content

```
<footer><p>Page Footer</p></footer>
</body>
</html>
```

3 Next, create a folder named "includes" in the **/htdocs** directory of your web server and save inside it the above documents as **header.html** and **footer.html** respectively

...cont'd

4 Create a CSS style sheet to present the header and footer content (and rules to present aspects of later examples)

```css
header > h1 { border-bottom : 1px dashed black ;
                font-style : italic ; font-size : x-large ; }
footer > p { border-top : 1px dashed black ;
                                font-style : italic ; }
table { border-spacing : 5px ; width : 530px ; }
th { color : #FFF ; background : #000 ; text-align : left ; }
td { border-bottom : 1px solid black ;
        padding : 3px ; background : #F0F0F0 ;
        text-align : left ; vertical-align :top ; }
p#err_msg { color : #F00 ; font-weight : bold ; }
```

style.css

5 Save the style sheet in the **/includes** folder you have created, alongside the HTML header and footer files

6 Finally, create a PHP script that sets the web page title and surrounds a form with header and footer content

```php
<?php
$page_title = 'PHP Include' ;
include ( 'includes/header.html' ) ;
echo '<form action="include.php" method="POST">
<p>Name: <input type="text" name="name"> </p>
<p>Email: <input type="text" name="email" ></p>
<p><input type="submit"></p></form>' ;
include ( 'includes/footer.html' ) ;
?>
```

include.php

7 Save the PHP script in your web server's **/htdocs** directory as **include.php** then open it via HTTP to see the page title set and a form surrounded by static content

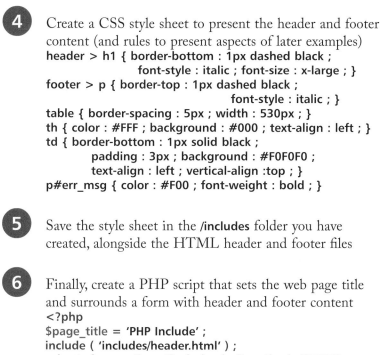

Hot tip

You can use your browser's View Source facility to see that the entire content has been effectively incorporated into a single web page.

Appending link data

PHP pre-defined "superglobal" variables, such as the **$_SERVER** array variable that stores the page request method and the **$_SESSION** array variable that stores user data across pages of a website until the user quits, are accessible in all scopes of any script.

Where an HTML form submits data using the **POST** method, the **$_POST** array stores the value of submitted form values in like-named array elements. So the value of a submitted field named "city" can be accessed using **$_POST['city']**.

Similarly, where data is submitted using the **GET** method, the **$_GET** array stores the value of submitted values in named array elements. So the value of a submitted data named "id" can be accessed using **$_GET['id']**. This is typically used to submit data to a script by appending a name=value pair to the URL in an HTML hyperlink anchor like this:

<a href="www.example.com/script.php?id=1">

The script receiving the data, nominated by the hyperlink, may then use the passed value to determine a response:

The **$_SESSION** superglobal will be used to store user details in Chapter 10.

link.php

 Create an HTML document containing a PHP script that seeks an element named "id" within the **$_GET** array

```php
<?php
if ( isset ( $_GET[ 'id' ] )
{
  # Handler statements to be inserted here (steps 2-3).
}
```

 Next, insert a handler statement to assign a passed value to a like-named PHP variable

```php
$id = $_GET[ 'id' ] ;
```

Now, insert a handler statement to output an appropriate response according to the value passed

```php
switch( $id )
{
  case 1 : echo 'Cow selected<hr>' ; break ;
  case 2 : echo 'Dog selected<hr>' ; break ;
  case 3 : echo 'Goat selected<hr>' ; break ;
}
```

4 Finally, add statements to display hyperlinks with appended values

```
echo '<h1>Select a buddy</h1>' ;
echo ' <p><a href="link.php?id=1">Cow</a> |' ;
echo ' <a href="link.php?id=2">Dog</a> | ' ;
echo ' <a href="link.php?id=3">Goat</a></p>' ;
?>
```

5 Save the PHP script in your web server's **/htdocs** directory as **link.php** then open it via HTTP and click the links to see the responses for the passed values

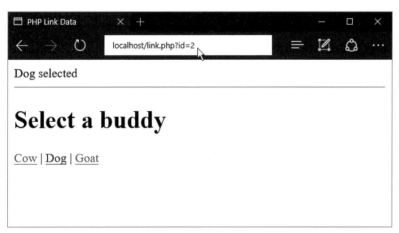

PHP also provides a **$_REQUEST** superglobal that contains the entire contents of the **$_POST** and **$_GET** arrays. This means that **$_POST['city']** is also accessible using **$_REQUEST['city']** but this should be avoided. Always use the specific array for the type of submission instead.

Notice that the passed name=value pair is visible in the browser address field.

Summary

- An HTML **<form>** tag's **action** attribute specifies the PHP script to handle the form submission, and its **method** attribute specifies how the data is sent to the script

- Form data submitted by the **POST** method gets automatically stored in the PHP superglobal **$_POST** array variable

- Elements of the **$_POST** array are named the same as the HTML form element containing each submitted value

- PHP can ensure that the user has entered data into submitted HTML form fields using the built-in **isset()** function

- The PHP **empty()** function checks whether a value has been entered into a form text field

- Format validation can be performed on submitted form data by the **is_numeric()** function and **preg_match()** function

- Data generated by PHP such as a timestamp created by the **date()** function can be submitted from hidden form fields

- The PHP superglobal **$_SERVER['REQUEST_METHOD']** array element stores the type of request made to load the page

- Sticky forms retain their field data simply by writing any submitted values back to the HTML input's **value** attribute

- The PHP **include()** and **require()** functions are used to incorporate other content and scripts within a web page

- Data submitted by the **GET** method gets automatically stored in the PHP superglobal **$_GET** array variable

- Hyperlinks can have name=value pairs appended to submit data to a script using the **GET** method

10 Preserving data

The **setcookie()** function can also accept further optional arguments to specify visible path, visible domain, https security, and visibility for http access only.

Submitting cookie data

Data entered by a user is frequently required across multiple pages of a website. User data can conveniently be stored in small "cookie" files on the client machine, so the user need not tediously enter the same data repeatedly. The PHP **setcookie()** function makes it easy to create a cookie by specifying three arguments:

setcookie(*name* , *value* , *expiry-time*) ;

When an HTML form is submitted to the server using the **POST** method, its field data is automatically assigned to the special PHP **$_POST** global array variable. A script can check for the presence of individual submission fields using a built-in PHP **isset()** function to seek an element of a specified HTML field name. When this confirms the field is indeed present, its name and value can usefully be stored in a cookie. This might be used to store username and password details for use across a website:

cookie_form.html

① Create an HTML document and add this form to its body section, specifying submission method and the name of a PHP submission-handler script
```
<form name = "entry" method = "POST"
                            action = "cookie_set.php">
<fieldset>
<legend>Enter Only AlphaNumeric Characters</legend>
Name : <input type = "text" name = "user" >
Password : <input type = "password" name = "pass" >
<br><br><input type = "submit" value = "Log In" >
</fieldset>
</form>
```

② Save the document in your web server's **/htdocs** directory as **cookie_form.html** then open the page via HTTP to see the form

Storing passwords in cookies is not the most secure method but is used here merely to demonstrate how to use cookies to store data.

![Browser window titled "PHP Cookie Form" at localhost/cookie_form.html showing a form with legend "Enter Only AlphaNumeric Characters", fields Name and Password, and a Log In button]

Setting cookies

Upon receiving a form submission, a PHP script can check for the presence of fields and might perform validation of their associated values. For example, the **ctype_alnum()** function could be used to simply confirm that the values only contain alphanumeric data.

Once validated, the **setcookie()** function can store the submitted fields' names and values. Additionally a hash conversion could be made of password values using the **md5()** function. On successful completion, the script can then relocate the browser to another page using the **header()** function to specify that page's URL:

The **ctype_alnum()** function returns true only if its argument contains alphanumeric characters.

1. Begin a PHP script with a function to handle failed validation attempts

```php
<?php
function reject( $entry )
{
  echo "Invalid $entry <br>" ;
  echo 'Please <a href="cookie_form.html">Log In</a>' ;
  exit() ;
}
```

cookie_set.php

2. Next, add a conditional test block to set two cookies for valid data, or call the function to handle failed attempts

```php
if( isset( $_POST[ 'user' ] ) )
{
  $user = trim( $_POST[ 'user' ] ) ;
  if( !ctype_alnum( $user ) ) { reject( 'User Name' ) ; }

  if( isset( $_POST[ 'pass' ] ) )
  {
    $pass = trim( $_POST[ 'pass' ] ) ;
    if( !ctype_alnum( $pass ) ) { reject( 'Password' ) ; }
    else
    {
      setcookie( 'user' , $user , time()+3600 ) ;
      setcookie( 'pass' , md5( $pass ) , time()+3600 ) ;
      header( 'Location: cookie_get.php' ) ;
    }
  }
}
else { header( 'Location: cookie_form.html' ) ; }
?>
```

Notice how the **time()** function is used here to get the current time, then one hour is added (in seconds) to set the cookie expiration time one hour ahead.

3. Save the document in your web server's **/htdocs** directory as **cookie_set.php** then see overleaf how to retrieve the stored cookie data

The final **else** statement will relocate to the HTML form page if the script URL is opened directly.

Getting cookies

Once cookies are set, they are automatically assigned to the special PHP **$_COOKIE** global array variable. A script can check for the presence of an individual cookie using the built-in PHP **isset()** function to seek a cookie of a specified name. When this confirms the cookie is indeed present, its value can usefully be assigned to a regular script variable. This might be used to retrieve a stored username for output on a page. Where a sought cookie is absent, the script can offer an alternative to the user:

cookie_get.php

1. Begin a PHP script with a test to find a cookie and retrieve data for output upon success

```php
<?php
if( isset( $_COOKIE[ 'user' ] ) )
{
  $user = $_COOKIE[ 'user' ] ;
  echo "<h1>Welcome $user !</h1><hr>" ;
  echo '<a href="cookie_data.php">View Cookie</a>' ;
}
```

2. Next, add alternative output for when the cookie is absent

```php
else
{
  echo 'Please <a href="cookie_form.html">Log In</a>' ;
}
?>
```

3. Save the document in your web server's **/htdocs** directory as **cookie_get.php**

4. Now open the HTML form **cookie_form.html** (created on page 146) via HTTP and push the submit button to see the login attempt fail validation, so no cookies are set

5 Click the hyperlink to return to the HTML form and enter a valid username, then push the submit button to see the login attempt fail validation again

PHP Cookie Set

localhost/cookie_set.php

Invalid Password
Please Log In

http://localhost/cookie_form.html

6 Return to the HTML form once more and enter a valid username and password to see validation succeed

PHP Cookie Form

localhost/cookie_form.html

Enter Only AlphaNumeric Characters

Name : Mike   Password : ••••••••

Log In

http://localhost/cookie_set.php

PHP Cookie Get

localhost/cookie_get.php

Welcome Mike !

View Cookie

7 See overleaf how to view data stored within cookies, using the **cookie_data.php** target of the hyperlink seen above

Don't forget

You can also return to the HTML form and enter a username or a password that includes non-alphanumeric characters, to see validation fail again.

Hot tip

Validation could be extended. For example, it may also allow underscore characters and might specify a minimum permissible password length.

Viewing cookie data

The special PHP **$_COOKIE** global array variable stores cookie names and values in an associative array of keys and values. Stored content can be viewed by looping through the array to see all names and values, or using the PHP **var_dump()** function:

cookie_data.php

Hot tip

You can call the **setcookie( )** function at any time to create a new cookie or overwrite an existing cookie.

1 Begin a PHP script with a test to find if any cookies are set and retrieve all stored names and values upon success

```php
<?php
if( count( $_COOKIE ) > 0 )
{
  echo '<dl> ' ;
  foreach( $_COOKIE as $key => $value )
  {
    echo "<dt>Key: $key" ;
    echo "<dd>Value: $value" ;
  }
  echo '</dl><hr>' ;
  var_dump( $_COOKIE ) ;
}
```

2 Next, add alternative output for when cookies are absent

```php
else
{
  echo 'Please <a href="cookie_form.html">Log In</a>' ;
}
?>
```

3 Save the document in your web server's **/htdocs** directory as **cookie_data.php**

4 Now, open the HTML form **cookie_form.html** (page 146) via HTTP and enter valid login data, then follow the link on **cookie_get.php** (page 148) to see cookie data

...cont'd

Key: user
        Value: Mike
Key: pass
        Value: 3a3795bb61d5377545b4f345ff223e3d

array(2) { ["user"]=> string(4) "Mike" ["pass"]=> string(32) "3a3795bb61d5377545b4f345ff223e3d" }

5   Open the **Settings** menu in your web browser and clear existing cookies that are stored on your system

6   Now, use the Refresh button in your browser to reload this page and see the alternative content – confirming that the cookie data has been removed

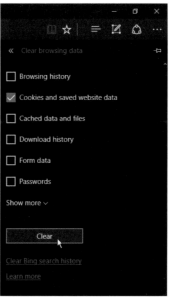

Hot tip

The PHP manual describes the removal of a cookie by setting its value to empty and its expiration date to the past. For example, **setcookie($_COOKIE['user'] , '' , time()-3600)**. Additionally, the **unset()** function can be used to destroy a specified variable.

Please Log In

Submitting session data

User data can be stored in cookies on the client computer only if the user chooses to allow cookies onto their system. Many users prefer to disallow cookies, however, to avoid tracking – but PHP provides a better alternative. With PHP, user data can be stored on the server using the special **$_SESSION** global array variable. In order for PHP sessions to work, each PHP page must call the built-in **session_start()** function at the top of the page – before any HTML tags! HTML form submissions to the server via the **POST** method assigns field data to the special PHP **$_POST** global array variable, and individual submission fields can be sought using the built-in PHP **isset()** function. When this confirms the field is present, its name and value can be stored in a session variable. This might be used to store a username and password details for use across a website, as an alternative to cookie storage:

Session variables will only be accessible to a PHP script if the **session_start()** function has been called at the top of the page.

session_form.html

1 Create an HTML document and add this form to its body section, specifying submission method and the name of a PHP submission-handler script

```
<form name = "entry" method = "POST"
                          action = "session_set.php">
<fieldset>
<legend>For Name : Enter Only Letters</legend>
Name : <input type="text" name="user" >
Password : <input type="password" name="pass" >
<p>For Password : Enter Only A-Z a-z 0-9 . _ (Minimum 8
Characters)</p> <input type="submit" value="Log In">
</fieldset>
</form>
```

2 Save the document in your web server's **/htdocs** directory as **session_form.html** then open the page via HTTP to see the form

PHP Session Form   ✕   +   —   ☐   ✕

← → ⟳   localhost/session_form.html   ≡   📝   ⚙   ⋯

For Name : Enter Only Letters

Name : [　　　　　　　　　]   Password : [　　　　　　　　　]

For Password : Enter Only A-Z a-z 0-9 . _ (Minimum 8 Characters)

[Log In]

Setting sessions

Upon receiving a form submission, a PHP script can check for the presence of fields and might perform validation of their associated values. For example, the **ctype_alpha()** function could be used to confirm they contain only letters, and the **preg_match()** function could be used to confirm a value matches a specified pattern. Once validated, the submitted fields' names and values can be assigned to elements of the **$_SESSION** global array variable. On successful completion, the script can relocate the browser to the next page using the **header()** function to specify that page's URL:

The **ctype_alpha()** function returns true only if its argument contains letters.

1. Add an initial PHP script to make sessions available
```php
<?php session_start(); ?>
```

session_set.php

2. Begin a PHP script to handle failed validation attempts
```php
<?php
function reject( $entry )
{
  echo "Invalid $entry <br>" ;
  echo 'Please <a href="session_form.html">Log In</a>' ;
  exit() ;
}
```

3. Add a conditional test block to set two cookies for valid data, or call the function to handle failed attempts
```php
if( isset( $_POST[ 'user' ] ) )
{
  $user = trim( $_POST[ 'user' ] ) ;
  if( !ctype_alpha( $user ) ) { reject( 'User Name' ) ; }
  if( isset( $_POST[ 'pass' ] ) )
  {
    $pass = trim( $_POST[ 'pass' ] ) ;
    if( !preg_match( '/^[A-Za-z0-9._]{8,}$/' , $pass ) )
    { reject( 'Password' ) ; }
    else
    {
      $_SESSION[ 'user' ] = $user ;
      $_SESSION[ 'pass' ] = $pass ;
      header( 'Location: session_get.php' ) ;
    }
  }
} else { header( 'Location: session_form.html' ) ; }
?>
```

The **preg_match()** function accepts a regular expression and a string argument. Regular expressions are beyond the remit of this book but you can precisely copy this example to allow the permissible password pattern described on the form. The password is left unencrypted in this example, to demonstrate later that the user password meets the specified requirements.

4. Save the document in your web server's **/htdocs** directory as **session_set.php** then see overleaf how to retrieve data

Getting sessions

Session data is accessible from the special **$_SESSION** global array variable after a call is made to the **session_start()** function. The PHP **isset()** function can seek an element of a specified name. When this confirms the element is present, its value can usefully be assigned to a regular script variable. This might be used to retrieve a stored username for output on a page. Where a sought element is absent, the script can offer an alternative to the user:

session_get.php

1. Add an initial PHP script to make sessions available
```
<?php session_start() ; ?>
```

2. Now, begin a PHP script to find a session variable and retrieve data for output upon success, or provide an alternative for when the session variable is absent
```
<?php
if( isset( $_SESSION[ 'user' ] ) )
{
  $user = $_SESSION[ 'user' ] ;
  echo "<h1>Welcome $user !</h1><hr>" ;
  echo '<a href="session_data.php">View Session</a>' ;
}
else
{ echo 'Please <a href="session_form.html">Log In</a>' ; }
?>
```

3. Save the document in your web server's **/htdocs** directory as **session_get.php**

4. Now, open the HTML form **session_form.html** (created on page 152) via HTTP and push the submit button to see the login attempt fail validation

5 Return to the HTML form and submit a valid username, to see the login attempt fail validation again

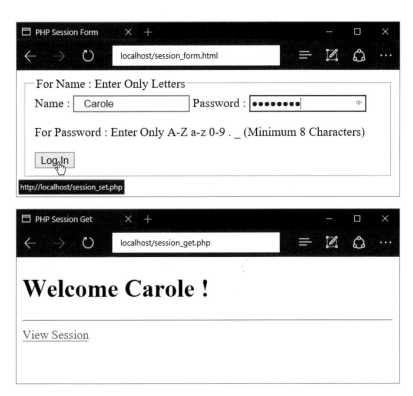

Don't forget

You can also return to the HTML form and enter a password below the minimum length or containing invalid characters to see validation fail again.

6 Return to the HTML form once more and enter a valid username and password to see validation succeed

Hot tip

Notice that the user in this example has added leading spaces before their name, but that's okay – these will be removed by the **trim()** function used in the **session_set.php** script.

7 See overleaf how to view data stored in session variables, using the **session_data.php** target of the link seen above

Don't forget

The uniqueness of each session allows variables to exist without conflict.

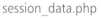

session_data.php

Hot tip

You can assign a new value to a session variable at any time to overwrite an existing stored value.

Viewing session data

The special PHP **$_SESSION** global array variable stores names and values in an associative array of keys and values. Stored content can be viewed by looping through the array to see all names and values, or using the PHP **var_dump()** function. Additionally, each session has a unique session ID number, which can be seen using the PHP **session_id()** function.

Set session variables can be removed by specifying their element name to the PHP **unset()** function, and a session can be completely terminated by calling the **session_destroy()** function:

1. Add an initial PHP script to make sessions available
```php
<?php session_start(); ?>
```

2. Now, begin a PHP script to remove session variables, terminate a session, and confirm termination
```php
<?php
function kill_session()
{
  unset( $_SESSION[ 'user' ] ) ;
  unset( $_SESSION[ 'pass' ] ) ;
  session_destroy() ;
  echo '<hr>Session Destroyed<br>' ;
  echo  'Session ID : '.session_id().'<br>' ;
  var_dump( $_SESSION ) ;
}
```

3. Now, add a test to find if any session variables are set and retrieve all stored names and values
```php
if( count( $_SESSION ) > 0 )
{
  echo '<dl> ' ;
  foreach( $_SESSION as $key => $value )
  {
    echo "<dt>Key: $key" ; echo "<dd>Value: $value" ;
  }
  echo '</dl><hr>' ;
  // Statements to be inserted here (step 4).
}
```

4. Insert statements to display the session ID and array, then call the function to terminate the session
```php
  echo 'Session ID : '.session_id().'<br>' ;
  var_dump( $_SESSION ) ;
  kill_session() ;
```

...cont'd

5 Add alternative output for when a session is absent

```
else
{ echo 'Please <a href="session_form.html">Log In</a>' ; }
?>
```

6 Save the document in your web server's **/htdocs** directory as **session_data.php**

7 Now, open the HTML form **session_form.html** (page 152) via HTTP and enter valid login data, then follow the link on **session_get.php** (page 154) to see session data

Hot tip

Notice that the password adheres to the permissible pattern.

8 Use the ⟳ Refresh button in your browser to reload this page to see the alternative "Please Log In" content

Summary

- The PHP **set_cookie()** function can be used to store user data on the client machine for use across the pages of a website

- There should be at least three arguments supplied to the **set_cookie()** function to specify name, value and expiry time

- HTML form submissions via the **POST** method automatically assign field data to the PHP **$_POST** global array variable

- The **isset()** function can seek an element of a specified HTML field name within the **$_POST** global array

- The **ctype_alnum()** function can be used to confirm a value only contains alphanumeric data for validation

- A hash conversion can be made of a password value using the **md5()** function for encryption

- The PHP **header()** function can specify a Location:URL to relocate the browser

- Once cookies are set, they are automatically assigned to the special PHP **$_COOKIE** global array variable

- User data can be stored on the server in the PHP **$_SESSION** global array variable as an alternative to cookie storage

- To use sessions, each PHP page must call the **session_start()** function at the top of the page before any HTML tags

- HTML field data submitted to the **$_POST** global array can be assigned to a **$_SESSION** global variable array element

- The **ctype_alpha()** function can be used to confirm a value only contains alphabetic letter data for validation

- The **preg_match()** function can be used to confirm a value matches a specified pattern for validation

- Each session has a unique session ID number, which can be seen using the PHP **session_id()** function

- Session variables can be removed using the **unset()** function and a session can be terminated using the **session_destroy()** function

- Stored content can be viewed using the **var_dump()** function and by looping through the **$_COOKIE** or **$_SESSION** arrays

11 Connecting databases

The MySQL Community Edition is available free at mysql.com/downloads/mysql

connect_db.php

Hot tip

This chapter assumes the MySQL database server is installed and configured for a user on the localhost server, with full privileges to use a database named "website_db". Further instruction and examples can be found in our companion book in this series **PHP & MySQL in easy steps**.

Making a connection

Connection to a MySQL database can be attempted from a standard PHP script. The script defines a variable named "dbc" (database connection) that gets assigned the value returned by calling a built-in **mysqli_connect()** function. This call requires four arguments to specify the host server, the MySQL username and password, and the database to connect. When the call succeeds, the **mysqli_connect()** function returns an "object" that represents the connection to the MySQL Server. The script looks like this:

```php
<?php

$dbc =
mysqli_connect( 'host' , 'user' , 'password' , 'database' )
OR die ( mysqli_connect_error() ) ;
mysqli_set_charset( $dbc , 'utf-8' ) ;
```

The object returned by a successful call to **mysqli_connect()** is very important as it is used as an argument in other PHP function calls that communicate with the MySQL Server. For example, in the above script it must be used as the first argument in the call to the **mysqli_set_charset()** function to identify the connection.

When the call to the **mysqli_connect()** function fails, the script branches to an alternative that calls the **die()** function. This is equivalent to calling **exit()** to immediately terminate the script. Optionally the **die()** function can accept a string argument that will be printed out as the scripts halts. In this case the string message is returned by the **mysqli_connect_error()** function that describes why the connection attempt failed.

As the connection script contains sensitive user details, it must not be placed alongside other PHP scripts in your web server's /**htdocs** directory. The **connect_db.php** script should instead be located in the parent directory of /**htdocs**, where it is not directly accessible but can be incorporated into other PHP scripts by a **require** statement, like this:

```php
<?php

require ( '../connect_db.php' ) ;

if ( mysqli_ping( $dbc ) )
{
  echo 'MySQL Server ' . mysqli_get_server_info( $dbc ) .
                          ' on ' . mysqli_get_host_info( $dbc ) ;
}
```

require.php

...cont'd

The files in your web server's directory structure should therefore be arranged in the hierarchy depicted below, so when you request the **require.php** script via HTTP, the **connect_db.php** script gets incorporated from its location in the parent directory, and the connection gets made to the MySQL Server.

Files that contain only pure PHP code, like both those listed here, should omit the PHP **?>** closing tag at the end of the file. This prevents accidental whitespace or new lines after the PHP closing tag, which may cause unwanted effects.

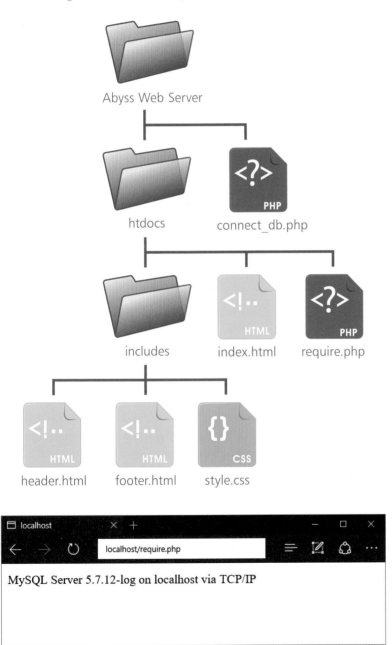

The connection script **connect_db.php** must be working successfully to connect to a MySQL database for the examples in this chapter.

```
🗖 localhost            × +                    —  □  ×
←  →  ○    localhost/require.php          ≡  🖍  ◌  ⋯

MySQL Server 5.7.12-log on localhost via TCP/IP
```

Creating a forum

User messages can be stored in a MySQL database table by a PHP script, so they may be subsequently retrieved for display in a forum page containing messages from various registered users. Typically a database table containing posted user messages might store the post ID, the user's first name and last name, the subject title, the message itself, and the date when posted:

Column Name:	Content Type:	Example:
post_id	Number	123
first_name	Text	Mike
last_name	Text	McGrath
subject	Text	Ice Cream
message	Text	Delicious on a hot day.
post_date	Date/Time	2016-07-24 12:30:00

Beware

MySQL database tables can only be created by the root MySQL user or another MySQL user that has been granted full access privileges.

Hot tip

You can discover how to fully use the Structured Query Language with databases from our companion book in this series entitled SQL in easy steps.

A database table of this design can be created using the Structured Query Language (SQL). The design of this database table simply requires that SQL **VARCHAR** or **TEXT** data types should be specified for those columns storing text. Post IDs should be positive SQL integer **INT** values that the table automatically allocates with SQL **AUTO_INCREMENT**, and the message posted timestamp should be stored as an SQL **DATETIME** value. All these items will be required to post a message to the database table so each column must have an SQL **NOT NULL** rule.

The SQL query command required to produce this design as a MySQL database table named "forum" can be issued at the prompt in the MySQL Command Line Client, or issued by running a PHP script in the web browser.

1 Begin a PHP script with a statement to connect to a database using the standard connection scripts described on the previous page

```php
<?php

require( '..\connect_db.php' ) ;
```

create_forum.php

2 Next, assign the SQL specifications of the table design to a variable

```php
$sql = 'CREATE TABLE IF NOT EXISTS forum ( '.
'post_id INT UNSIGNED NOT NULL AUTO_INCREMENT ,'.
'first_name VARCHAR(20) NOT NULL ,'.
'last_name VARCHAR(40) NOT NULL ,'.
'subject VARCHAR(60) NOT NULL ,'.
'message TEXT NOT NULL ,'.
'post_date DATETIME NOT NULL ,'.
'PRIMARY KEY ( post_id ) ) ' ;
```

Hot tip

The SQL **VARCHAR** data type specifies a character length, whereas the **TEXT** data type accommodates up to 65,535 characters.

3 Now, add a test to report whether the table was created successfully, or describe the error on failure

```php
if( mysqli_query( $dbc , $sql ) === TRUE )
{
  echo 'Table "forum" created successfully' ;
}
else
{
  echo 'Error creating table : '.mysqli_error( $dbc ) ;
}
```

Hot tip

The **mysqli_query()** function executes the SQL query, whereas the **mysqli_error()** function will provide a report if an error occurs.

4 Remember to close the database connection when done

```php
mysqli_close( $dbc ) ;
```

5 Save the document in your web server's **/htdocs** directory as **create_forum.php** then open the page via HTTP to create the forum table

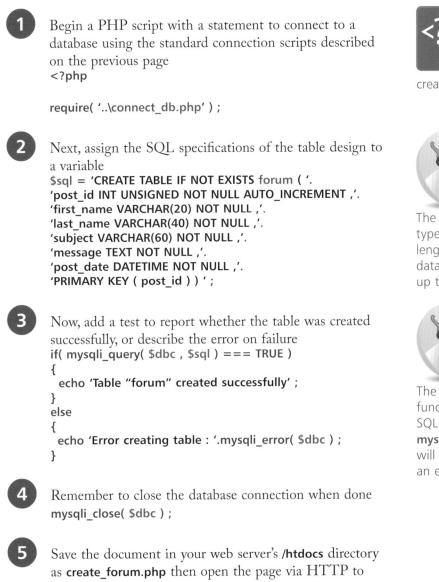

Providing the page

A forum page can be created to display previously posted messages retrieved from the MySQL 'forum' database table, created on the previous page. Forum messages can be displayed between the page header and footer, together with a hyperlink to another page where the user can post a new forum message. If the forum database contains no previously posted content, the script can simply advise that there are currently no messages.

The PHP **mysqli_query()** function can make an SQL query to retrieve the database table content, and the **mysqli_num_rows()** function can discover how many table rows are in the result. When table rows are found in the result, the **mysqli_fetch_array()** function can be used to fetch an associative array of rows and data in each column by specifying the result and **MYSQLI_ASSOC** constant as arguments:

forum.php

 Begin a PHP script with a statement to set the page title
<?php

$page_title = 'PHP Forum' ;

 Next, add a statement to include a page header
include ('includes/header.html') ;

3 Add a statement to open the database connection
require ('..\connect_db.php') ;

4 Retrieve all messages from the database table and assign them to a variable
$sql = 'SELECT * FROM forum' ;
$result = mysqli_query($dbc , $sql) ;

 Test whether the database table is empty and display an appropriate advisory comment
if (mysqli_num_rows($result) > 0)
{
  // Statements to be inserted here (step 6).
}
else
{
  echo '<p>There are currently no messages.</p>' ;
}

Don't forget

Columns are returned as an associative array in which the row name is the key for each value in that column.

6 Next, insert statements to write a table displaying all messages retrieved from the database table if any are found

```
echo '<table><tr><th>Posted By</th>
<th>Subject</th><th id="msg">Message</th></tr>' ;

while ( $row = mysqli_fetch_array( $result , MYSQLI_ASSOC ) )
{
  echo '<tr><td>'.
  $row[ 'first_name' ].' '.
  $row[ 'last_name' ].'<br>'.
  $row[ 'post_date' ].'</td><td>'.
  $row[ 'subject' ].'</td><td>'.
  $row[ 'message' ].'</td></tr>';
}

echo '</table>' ;
```

Hot tip

Database table rows are returned into the array having the row name as the array index. The cells on the HTML table row will be populated by the data contained in the columns on a row of the database forum table.

7 After the test block, add a statement to create a hyperlink to a "Post Message" page

```
echo '<p><a href="post.php">Post Message</a></p>' ;
```

8 Now, add a statement to close the database connection

```
mysqli_close( $dbc ) ;
```

9 Add a final statement to include a page footer

```
include ( 'includes/footer.html' ) ;
?>
```

10 Save the document in your web server's **/htdocs** directory as **forum.php** then open the page via HTTP to see the forum page

```
PHP Forum        ×  +            —   □   ×
←  →  ↻    localhost/forum.php        ≡  📝  ♻  ...

Page Header
--------------------------------------------------------------


There are currently no messages.

Post Message
--------------------------------------------------------------
Page Footer
```

Don't forget

The HTML header and footer inclusions are demonstrated in the example on page 140.

Supplying a form

Having completed the PHP script to display posted forum messages, described on the previous page, we can now create a PHP script to allow the user to post new messages. This can simply provide an HTML form with fields for usernames, the subject title, and the message body itself:

post.php

 Begin a PHP script with a statement to set the page title
```
<?php

$page_title = 'PHP Post Message' ;
```

 Now, add a statement to include a page header
```
include ( 'includes/header.html' ) ;
```

 Add a statement to display the form
```
echo '<form action="process.php"
        method="POST" accept-charset="utf-8">

First Name : <input name="first_name" type="text">
Last Name : <input name="last_name" type="text">

<p>Subject :<br>
<input name="subject" type="text" size="64"></p>
<p>Message :<br>
<textarea name="message" rows="5" cols="50">
</textarea></p>
<p><input type="submit" value="Submit"></p>

</form>' ;
```

 Next, add a statement to create a hyperlink to the Forum page
```
echo '<p>
<a href="forum.php">Forum</a></p>' ;
```

 Add a final statement to include a page footer
```
include ( 'includes/footer.html' ) ;
?>
```

6 Save this script in your web server's **/htdocs** directory as **post.php** then follow the hyperlink on the Forum page to see this message form page

Hot tip

Notice that the form **action** attribute nominates a submission handler named **process.php** – this is listed on page 168.

166

...cont'd

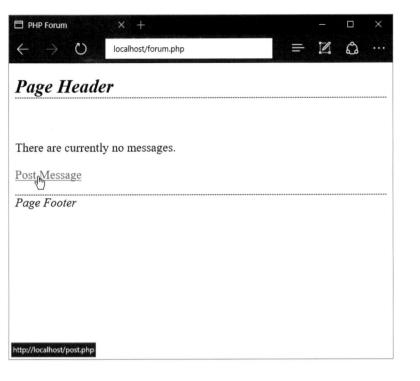

Hot tip

In practice, users of a forum may have first registered their names. In that case, those names could also be stored in a database table for recall later – but usernames will be submitted by the HTML form in this example, for simplicity.

Don't forget

The Post Message page provides a hyperlink back to the Forum page, should the user wish to return there.

Processing messages

Having completed the PHP script to supply a form to post new forum messages, described on the previous pages, you can now create a PHP script to process the submitted messages.

The script to process the HTML form can ensure that all form fields are not empty for simple validation. The **trim()** function can be used to strip whitespace and the **empty()** function can be used to test for empty string submissions.

Once the form input is found to be valid, the script can then store the submitted message in the MySQL "forum" database table. If the attempt to post the message succeeds the forum page can be loaded to display the messages, or upon failure an error message can be displayed:

process.php

Don't forget

This script is nominated by the form in **post.php** to process its submitted user data messages. The form is not "sticky" though – so any entered field data is not retained if the user must return to the form to complete an empty input field.

1 Begin a PHP script with a statement to set the page title
```
<?php

$page_title = 'PHP Process Error' ;
```

2 Next, add a statement to include a page header
```
include ( 'includes/header.html' ) ;
```

 Now, add an exit function to display a notification and a link to return to the post page if validation fails
```
function fail( $str )
{
  echo "<p>Please enter a $str.</p>" ;
  echo '<p><a href="post.php">Post Message</a>' ;
  include ( 'includes/footer.html' ) ;
  exit() ;
}
```

 Add a test to ensure the form has been submitted
```
if( isset( $_POST[ 'message' ] ) )
{

// Statements to be inserted here (step 5).

// Statements to be inserted here (step 6).

// Statements to be inserted here (step 7).


}
```

5 Insert tests to ensure the user has filled in all form fields

```
if ( !empty( trim( $_POST[ 'first_name' ] ) ) )
{ $first_name = addslashes( $_POST[ 'first_name' ] ) ; }
else { fail( 'First Name' ) ; }

if ( !empty( trim( $_POST[ 'last_name' ] ) ) )
{ $last_name = addslashes(  $_POST[ 'last_name' ] ) ; }
else { fail( 'Last Name' ) ; }

if ( !empty( trim( $_POST[ 'subject' ] ) ) )
{ $subject = addslashes( $_POST[ 'subject' ] ) ; }
else { fail( 'Subject' ) ; }

if ( !empty( trim( $_POST[ 'message' ] ) ) )
{ $message = addslashes( $_POST[ 'message' ] ) ; }
else { fail( 'Message' ) ; }
```

Beware

Notice that the PHP **addslashes()** function is used here to escape apostrophes and quotes.

6 When validation succeeds, open the database connection

```
require ( '../connect_db.php' ) ;
```

7 Now, insert statements to add the submitted HTML form field values into the MySQL "forum" database table

```
$sql = "INSERT INTO forum
( first_name, last_name, subject, message, post_date )
VALUES
('$first_name', '$last_name','$subject', '$message', NOW() )" ;

$result = mysqli_query ( $dbc , $sql ) ;
```

Hot tip

NOW() is a MySQL function, which returns a datetime value that is the current timestamp.

169

8 Finally, insert a statement to report a failure error or relocate the browser to the forum page on success

```
if ( mysqli_affected_rows( $dbc ) != 1 )
{
  echo '<p>Error</p>'.mysqli_error( $dbc ) ;
  mysqli_close( $dbc ) ;
}
else
{
  mysqli_close( $dbc ) ;
  header( 'Location: forum.php' ) ;
}
```

Hot tip

This script supplies its own error messages if it finds empty form fields, or a MySQL error message if the data cannot be added to the database table.

9 Save this script in your web server's **/htdocs** directory as **process.php**, then submit the form without entries in all fields to see the script display error messages

Confirming success

It's now time to test the message board process to ensure that validation performs correctly, and posted messages appear on the Forum page:

 Open the Post Message page, then complete all fields and submit the form to see the message appear on the forum

The "Posted By" details are retrieved from the first_name, last_name, and post_date columns of the MySQL "forum" database table.

2 Next, return to the Post Message page then attempt to post a message with no Subject entry to see an error

| PHP Process Error | × | + | | — | □ | × |

← → ⟳ localhost/process.php ≡ 🖊 ⬡ ⋯

Page Header

Please enter a Subject.

Post Message

Page Footer

http://localhost/post.php

Hot tip

You can stop the MySQL Server service and post a message to see the MySQL error report.

3 Return to the Post Message page and post more messages as different users to see them get added to the forum

| PHP Forum | × | + | | — | □ | × |

← → ⟳ localhost/forum.php ≡ 🖊 ⬡ ⋯

Page Header

Posted By	Subject	Message
Mike McGrath 2016-04-26 14:53:09	Ice Cream	Delicious on a hot day.
Charlie Smith 2016-04-26 14:57:53	Biscuits	Best dipped in coffee.
Heather Jones 2016-04-26 14:58:42	Toast	Always falls buttered side down
Tony Brown 2016-04-26 14:59:22	Fruit	I eat it five times a day
Alice White 2016-04-26 14:59:58	Chocolate	Naughty, but nice!

Post Message

Page Footer

Hot tip

New forum messages are added to the bottom of the table here but the order could be reversed by adding a **SORT** clause to the SQL query.

Summary

- A PHP script can connect to a MySQL database using the **mysqli_connect()** function to specify the host server, username, user password, and database name as its arguments

- The **mysqli_connect()** function returns a database connection object, which can be supplied as the argument to other functions, such as the **mysqli_set_charset()** function

- The **die()** function is equivalent to calling the **exit()** function to terminate the script

- The **mysqli_connect_error()** function returns an error message if a connection attempt fails, and can be specified as the argument to the **die()** function, to be called as the script halts

- It is recommended to place a connection script outside the regular **/htdocs** directory for security and incorporate it into other scripts, when needed, using a **require** statement

- The **mysqli_ping()** function can verify connection to a specified database, then information can be retrieved using **mysqli_get_server_info()** and **mysqli_get_host_info()**

- The **mysqli_query()** function attempts to execute a SQL query on a specified database object and the **mysqli_error()** function can be used to describe the cause of a failed attempt

- Database connections should always be closed when they are no longer required by calling the **mysqli_close()** function

- When a database query succeeds, the **mysqli_num_rows()** function can reveal the total number of rows retrieved

- The **mysqli_fetch_array()** function can create an associative array of rows and data from a successful query result

- The PHP **empty()** function can be used to test a posted HTML form field to discover if it is empty

- A row of data can be added to a MySQL database table, using the **mysqli_query()** function, then a confirmation test can be made using the **mysqli_affected_rows()** function

- The browser can be relocated to a new page using the **header()** function to specify a **'Location:URL'** argument

12 Adding Web Services

Loading data

There are many "Web Services" available online, which provide free data that can usefully be incorporated in your own web pages. Typical examples might supply live stock prices, the latest news stories, or current weather conditions.

Most Web Services offer to supply data in the XML (eXtensible Markup Language) file format. This is designed to be both human-readable and machine-readable and is not reliant upon any single platform. For example, a Java program can send XML data over the internet to a .NET application, and vice versa.

XML looks very much like HTML, but with XML you make up your own element names. The element tags surround content and may include attributes, as with HTML. It is important that each element has both opening and closing tags, and that elements are correctly nested for the XML document to be "well-formed".

Beware

All XML documents must begin with an XML file type declaration – like the one shown here on line one.

catalog.xml

Hot tip

The **catalog.xml** file shown here will be used in the next few examples to demonstrate how to load XML data and how to access element values or attribute values.

```
≡     Code Writer                                    ⤢   —   □   ✕
 1    <?xml version="1.0" encoding="UTF-8"?>
 2    <catalog>
 3      <book>
 4        <title cover="images/c.jpg">C Programming</title>
 5        <category>Compiled</category>
 6      </book>
 7      <book>
 8        <title cover="images/java.jpg">Java</title>
 9        <category>Compiled</category>
10      </book>
11      <book>
12        <title cover="images/jq.jpg">jQuery</title>
13        <category>Interpreted</category>
14      </book>
15      <book>
16        <title cover="images/php.jpg">PHP</title>
17        <category>Interpreted</category>
18      </book>
19      <book>
20        <title cover="images/sql.jpg">SQL</title>
21        <category>Interpreted</category>
22      </book>
23    </catalog>

Ln 1        Col 1        •••    <                              >
```

PHP provides an XML parser called "SimpleXML" that can load an XML document into memory as a hierarchical tree structure. The **simplexml_load_file()** function requires the XML file name and path to transform the document into a data structure comprising "SimpleXMLElement" objects. The data structure can then be explored using the **var_dump()** function.

catalog.php

1 Begin a PHP script with a statement to set a page title and to preserve text formatting
```php
<?php
echo '<title>PHP SimpleXML</title><pre>' ;
```

2 Next, add a statement to load the XML data or quit
```php
$xml = simplexml_load_file( 'catalog.xml' )
or die( 'Unable to load data!' ) ;
```

3 Now, display all the SimpleXMLElement objects
```php
var_dump( $xml ) ;
```

4 Save the document in your web server's **/htdocs** directory as **catalog.php**, alongside the **catalog.xml** file, then open the page via HTTP to see the SimpleXMLElement objects

```
┌─────────────────────────────────────────────────────────┐
│ □ PHP SimpleXML        × +            —  □  ×            │
│ ←  →  ↻   localhost/catalog.php      ≡ 🖉 ◌ ···           │
├─────────────────────────────────────────────────────────┤
object(SimpleXMLElement)#1 (1) {
  ["book"]=>
  array(5) {
    [0]=>
    object(SimpleXMLElement)#2 (2) {
      ["title"]=>
      string(13) "C Programming"
      ["category"]=>
      string(8) "Compiled"
    }
    [1]=>
    object(SimpleXMLElement)#3 (2) {
      ["title"]=>
      string(4) "Java"
      ["category"]=>
      string(8) "Compiled"
    }
    [2]=>
    object(SimpleXMLElement)#4 (2) {
      ["title"]=>
      string(6) "jQuery"
      ["category"]=>
      string(11) "Interpreted"
    }
    [3]=>
    object(SimpleXMLElement)#5 (2) {
      ["title"]=>
      string(3) "PHP"
      ["category"]=>
      string(11) "Interpreted"
    }
    [4]=>
    object(SimpleXMLElement)#6 (2) {
      ["title"]=>
      string(3) "SQL"
      ["category"]=>
      string(11) "Interpreted"
    }
  }
}
```

Hot tip

Notice that this data structure depicts an array named "book" that has five array elements – corresponding to the five XML <book> elements.

Don't forget

The ubiquitous nature of XML makes it ideal to transport data across the internet.

Getting nodes

The data structure contained in a SimpleXML object describes a parent-child relationship between outer and inner XML elements. Each member of the data structure is known as a "node". The top-level nodes are direct child descendants of the SimpleXML object itself, so can be referenced using the object name, **->** object operator, and child node name. For example, **$object->child**. A child of the child node (grandchild) can be referenced by adding a further **->** object operator, and the grandchild node name, such as **$object->child->grandchild** and so on for each further generation:

nodes.php

Hot tip

As there are five "book" nodes on the same hierarchical level, in this example they are created as an array. Each node can therefore be individually referenced using its node name and array index number.

1 Begin a PHP script with a statement to set a page title
```
<?php
echo '<title>PHP SimpleXML</title>' ;
```

2 Add a statement to load the XML data or quit
```
$xml = simplexml_load_file( 'catalog.xml' )
or die( 'Unable to load data!' ) ;
```

3 Next, retrieve the content of the "title" element that is a child of the first "book" element
```
echo 'First book : '.
        $xml->book[0]->title.' in easy steps<br>' ;
```

4 Now, retrieve the content of the "category" element that is a child of the first "book" element
```
echo 'Language category : '.$xml->book[0]->category ;
```

5 Save the document in your web server's **/htdocs** directory as **nodes.php**, alongside the **catalog.xml** file, then open the page via HTTP to see the node content

Looping through nodes

The SimpleXML object provides methods to work with the data contained within its data structure. Usefully, its **children()** method returns all child nodes and can be used to loop through the nodes to retrieve each node's content:

  1 Begin a PHP script with a statement to set a page title
```php
<?php
echo '<title>PHP SimpleXML</title>' ;
```

2 Add a statement to load the XML data or quit
```php
$xml = simplexml_load_file( 'catalog.xml' )
or die( 'Unable to load data!' ) ;
```

3 Next, initialize an iteration counter at zero
```php
$counter = 0 ;
```

4 Now, add a loop to increment the counter and to display all "title" and "category" child node content
```php
foreach( $xml->children() as $book )
{
  $counter++ ;
  echo 'Book '.$counter.' : ' ;
  echo $book->title.
  ' in easy steps ['.$book->category.']<hr>' ;
}
```

5 Save the document in your web server's **/htdocs** directory as **nodes-loop.php**, alongside the **catalog.xml** file, then open the page via HTTP to see all node content

nodes-loop.php

Nested **foreach** loops can be used to traverse child nodes of each descendant generation.

177

PHP SimpleXML

localhost/nodes-loop.php

Book 1 : C Programming in easy steps [Compiled]

Book 2 : Java in easy steps [Compiled]

Book 3 : jQuery in easy steps [Interpreted]

Book 4 : PHP in easy steps [Interpreted]

Book 5 : SQL in easy steps [Interpreted]

Getting attributes

Values contained within attributes of a SimpleXMLElement object can be referenced by stating the attribute name, within quotes, between brackets following the node name. For example, **$object->child['feature']** accesses the value within an attribute named "feature" of a top-level "child" element:

attribs.php

1 Begin a PHP script with a statement to set a page title
```
<?php
echo '<title>PHP SimpleXML</title>' ;
```

2 Add a statement to load the XML data or quit
```
$xml = simplexml_load_file( 'catalog.xml' )
or die( 'Unable to load data!' ) ;
```

3 Next, retrieve the content of the "title" element that is a child of the first "book" element
```
echo 'First book : '.
        $xml->book[0]->title.' in easy steps<br>' ;
```

4 Now, display the value of the "cover" attribute of the "title" element, that is a child of the first "book" element
```
echo 'Cover : '.$xml->book[0]->title['cover'].'<br>' ;
```

5 Use the value retrieved in the previous step to display a cover image for the first "book" element
```
echo '<img src="'.$xml->book[0]->title['cover'].'">' ;
```

6 Save the document in your web server's **/htdocs** directory as **nodes.php**, alongside the **catalog.xml** file, then open the page via HTTP to see the attribute value and image

Notice that each attribute value here is the path and filename to an image in a directory at **/htdocs/images**.

Looping through attributes

The SimpleXML object **children()** method can once again be used to loop through nodes and retrieve the value in a specified attribute of a particular node on each iteration:

1 Begin a PHP script with a statement to set a page title
```
<?php
echo '<title>PHP SimpleXML</title>' ;
```

2 Add a statement to load the XML data or quit
```
$xml = simplexml_load_file( 'catalog.xml' )
or die( 'Unable to load data!' ) ;
```

3 Next, initialize an iteration counter at zero
```
$counter = 0 ;
```

4 Now, add a loop to increment the counter and to display its value, then retrieve an attribute value on each iteration to display an image
```
foreach( $xml->children() as $book )
{
  $counter++ ;
  echo ' '.$counter.': ' ;
  echo '<img src="'.$book->title['cover'].'">' ;
}
```

5 Save the document in your web server's **/htdocs** directory as **attribs-loop.php**, alongside the **catalog.xml** file, then open the page via HTTP to see the counter and image displayed on each iteration of the loop

attribs-loop.php

Hot tip

A SimpleXMLElement object also provides an **attributes()** method that returns an associative array of all attribute names and values within an element. For example, **$obj->child->attributes()**

179

You can discover more about RSS online at **rssboard.org** and can enter the URL of any RSS feed into their validator to see its XML elements.

Including feeds

With the ability to access data from XML documents within PHP scripts, as described on the previous pages, we can easily incorporate data from external sources. Many Web Services are offered as freely available RSS (Rich Site Summary/Really Simple Syndication) feeds. An online search for "rss feed directory" will provide a number of websites where links to free feeds are categorized. RSS feeds deliver regularly updated data in XML format.

The Yahoo! Developer Network (YDN) offer lots of free RSS feeds with helpful information at **real.developer.yahoo.com/rss** The only requirement for their use is that you must include an attribution to Yahoo! on the web page where they are displayed.

One of the free RSS feeds offered by Yahoo! provides regularly updated content describing entertainment news items, and can be found at **http://news.yahoo.com/rss/entertainment** This is delivered to the web browser as an XML file and can be displayed by the browser with buttons added to the outer elements, which you can click to expand (+) or collapse (-) nested elements.

RSS is a dialect of XML in which all documents must have a top-level **<rss>** element containing a **<channel>** element. Data is enclosed within inner elements:

The tags highlighted here can be used to retrieve the data of most interest. The item tags shown collapsed each also contain title, description, link and "pubDate" elements describing each item.

```
Y news.yahoo.com         ×   +                           —   □   ×
←  →  ↻          news.yahoo.com/rss/entertainment        ≡  ⊠  ◌  ...

<?xml version="1.0" encoding="UTF-8"?>
- <rss version="2.0" xmlns:media="http://search.yahoo.com/mrss/">
  - <channel>
        <title>Entertainment News Headlines — Yahoo! News</title>
        <link>http://news.yahoo.com/entertainment/</link>
        <description>Get the latest entertainment news</description>
        <language>en-US</language>
        <copyright>Copyright (c) 2016 Yahoo! Inc.</copyright>
        <pubDate>Tue, 04 Nov 2014 12:59:01 -0500</pubDate>
        <ttl>5</ttl>
      - <item>
            <title>McCartney: crisis inspired 'Blackbird'</title>
            <description>NORTH LITTLE ROCK, Ark. (AP) — Paul McCartney
              says he met with two of the women who inspired
              the Beatles' hit song "Blackbird."</description>
            <link>http://news.yahoo.com/151801455.html</link>
            <pubDate>Mon, 02 May 2016 11:18:01 -0400</pubDate>
            <source url="http://www.ap.org/">Associated Press</source>
            <guid isPermaLink="false">crisis-inspired-blackbird</guid>
        </item>
      + <item>
      + <item>
      + <item>
      + <item>
    </channel>
</rss>
```

...cont'd

rss.php

1 Begin a PHP script with a statement to load XML data from the RSS feed or quit
```
<?php
$url = 'http://rss.news.yahoo.com/rss/entertainment' ;
$xml =
simplexml_load_file( $url ) or die( 'Unable to load data!' ) ;
```

2 Next, add a statement to load a page header file
```
include( 'includes/rss-header.html' ) ;
```

3 Now, display each news item, then a page footer
```
foreach ( $xml->channel->item as $item ) {
echo '<a href="'.$item->link.'">' .$item->title.'</a>' ;
echo '<br><small>'.$item->pubDate.'</small><br>' ;
echo $item->description . '<hr>' ; }
include( 'includes/rss-footer.html' ) ;
```

4 Save the document in your web server's **/htdocs** directory as **rss.php** then open the page via HTTP to see the news

Don't forget

The terms of use for Yahoo! RSS feeds require you to display an attribution on your page.

Setting parameters

Some Web Services provide a static URL, like the Yahoo! RSS feed in the previous example, that simply delivers XML data pre-determined by the content supplier. Other Web Services provide a more flexible API (Application Programming Interface) that allows you to specify parameters in the URL request to determine what data you will receive, and in which format.

OpenWeatherMap has a free Current Weather Data API that can be found at **http://api.openweathermap.org/data/2.5/weather** The Current Weather Data API allows you to request weather data in many forms. The parameters provided by this API include:

- **q** = city name (or city name, country code)

- **units** = metric (celsius), imperial (fahrenheit), or standard (kelvin, the default) temperature scale

- **mode** = xml, html, or json (the default) format

- **appid** = required authorization key, supplied free upon registration at OpenWeatherMap

The parameters and required = values are appended to the OpenWeatherMap URL after a **?** and are separated by **&**.

The response from OpenWeatherMap can be delivered as an XML file that may be written into the web server's **/htdocs** folder using the PHP **asXml()** function to specify a filename. This can be examined in the web browser to discover the nature of the data retrieved, the XML element names, attribute names and structure:

Discover more about OpenWeatherMap at **openweathermap.org** and sign up to receive your own ID key.

params.php

1. Begin a PHP script by assigning string values to four variables, which will be used to set response parameters
```php
<?php
$city = 'New York' ;
$units = 'imperial' ;
$mode = 'xml' ;
$id = '28df3c64f387cf55026e0de3fb8beaa4' ;
```

2. Next, add a statement to build a request string using specified parameter values
```php
$request =
'http://api.openweathermap.org/data/2.5/weather?'.
'q='.$city.'&units='.$units.'&mode='.$mode.'&APPID='.$id ;
```

3 Now, add a statement to load XML data using the request string parameters, or quit

```
$xml = simplexml_load_file( $request )
or die( 'Unable to load data!' ) ;
```

4 When a response is received, attempt to write the content as an XML file in the web server's **/htdocs** directory

```
try
{
  $xml->asXml( 'params.xml' ) ;
  // Statement to be inserted here (step 5).
}
catch( Exception $e )
{
  echo 'Error : '.$e->getMessage() ;
}
```

params.xml

5 Insert a statement to relocate the browser to view the newly created XML document

```
header( 'Location: params.xml' ) ;
```

6 Save the PHP script in your web server's **/htdocs** directory as **params.php** then open the page via HTTP to examine the XML content of the retrieved response

The response will only contain weather data for prevailing conditions.

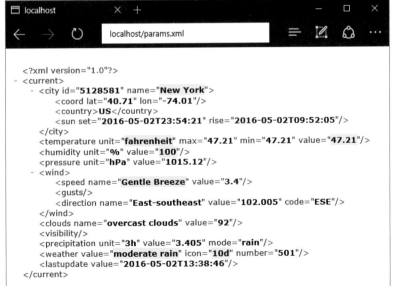

The data highlighted here is that of most interest. It can be retrieved using each containing element name and attribute name.

Selecting components

Having examined the response data retrieved from OpenWeatherMap on the previous page, selected components can be dynamically incorporated into a PHP sticky form XML App:

PHP

weather.php

1 Begin a PHP script by loading a page header file to provide a banner image
```
<?php
include( 'includes/weather-header.html' ) ;
```

2 Next, add a conditional test to see if the page has been opened by form submission
```
if( $_SERVER[ 'REQUEST_METHOD' ] == 'POST' )
{
  // Statements to be inserted here (steps 3-6).
}
```

Hot tip

Notice that a default city value is assigned in case the form is submitted without user input.

3 Inside the conditional test block, assign parameter string values to four variables
```
$city = ( empty( $_POST[ 'city' ] ) ) ? "New York"
        : $_POST[ 'city' ] ;
$units = 'imperial' ;
$mode = 'xml' ;
$id = '28df3c64f387cf55026e0de3fb8beaa4' ;
```

4 Next, inside the conditional test block, insert a statement to build a request string using specified parameter values
```
$request =
'http://api.openweathermap.org/data/2.5/weather?'.
'q='.$city.'&units='.$units.'&mode='.$mode.'&APPID='.$id ;
```

5 Now, inside the conditional test block insert a statement to load XML data using the parameters, or quit
```
$xml = simplexml_load_file( $request )
or die( 'Unable to load data!' ) ;
```

Hot tip

The value of the **icon** attribute is the name of a PNG image file. When concatenated to the path and **.png** file extension, it provides an appropriate weather image.

6 Finally, insert statements to output retrieved data
```
$icon = 'http://openweathermap.org/img/w/'.
        $xml->weather[ 'icon' ].'.png' ;
echo '<h1>Today in '.$xml->city[ 'name' ] ;
echo ' it\'s '.$xml->weather[ 'value' ].
        '<img src='.$icon.'></h1>' ;
echo '<ul><li>Temperature : '.$xml->temperature['value'] ;
echo '&deg; '.$xml->temperature[ 'unit' ] ;
echo '<li>Wind : '.$xml->wind->speed[ 'name' ] ;
echo '<li>Humidity : '.$xml->humidity['value'].'&#37;</ul>' ;
```

7 After the test block, add statements to create a form
```
echo '<form method="POST" action="weather.php">' ;
echo '<fieldset><legend>Enter City Name</legend>' ;
echo '<input type="text" name="city">' ;
echo '<input type="submit"
        name="submission" value = "Get Weather">' ;
echo '</fieldset></form>' ;
```

The **action** attribute specifies this same script filename to make the form sticky.

8 Finally, in the script, load a page footer file to display icons denoting the technologies employed by this app
```
include( 'includes/weather-footer.html' ) ;
```

9 Save the PHP script in your web server's **/htdocs** directory as **weather.php** then open the page via HTTP and submit the form to see weather for the default New York location. Enter another city name and re-submit to see that weather report

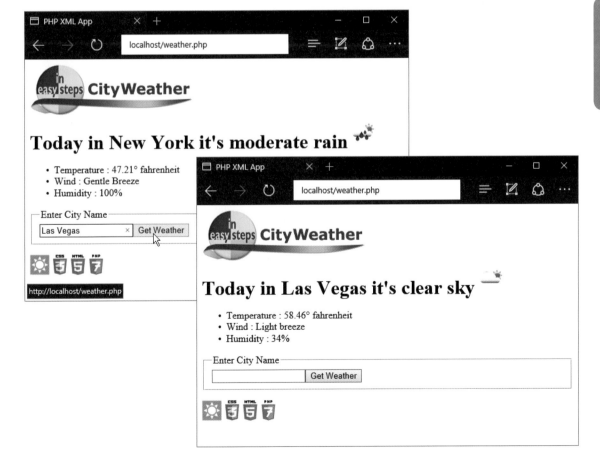

Summary

- XML elements must each have an opening and closing tag and be correctly nested to be well-formed

- PHP has an XML parser called SimpleXML that can load an XML document into memory as a hierarchical tree structure

- The **simplexml_load_file()** function creates a data structure of SimpleXMLElement objects

- The data structure of a SimpleXML object describes a parent-child relationship between outer and inner XML elements

- Each member of a SimpleXML data structure is a node

- Top-level nodes are direct child descendants of the SimpleXML object itself

- Nodes can be referenced using the **->** object operator to address each generation of the hierarchical tree structure

- The **children()** method returns all child nodes and can be used to loop through tree nodes to retrieve each node's content

- Attributes can be referenced by stating the attribute name, within quotes, between brackets following the node name

- RSS feeds deliver regularly updated data in XML format

- RSS is a dialect of XML in which all documents must have a top-level **<rss>** element containing a **<channel>** element

- Web Services may provide a static URL or an API that allows you to specify parameters in the URL request

- Parameter values are specified by an = character and are appended to a URL after a **?** and are separated by **&**

- A SimpleXML object can be written as an XML file on the server using the **asXml()** function

- Selected components of a SimpleXML object can be dynamically incorporated into a PHP application

Index

M

N

O

P

Q

R

S

T

U